The Unknowns Rising

When God Unleashes the New Billionaire Class

Arturo Serna Jr.

Cosmos Renewed

Cosmos Renewed Publishing

Scripture Credits
Unless otherwise noted, Scripture quotations are taken from the Holy Bible, New International Version®, NIV®. Copyright © 1973, 1978, 1984, 2011 by Biblica, Inc.™ Used by permission of Zondervan. All rights reserved worldwide.

Design Credits
Cover design by Christy McFerren
Interior design and layout by Arturo Serna Jr. via Atticus

Disclaimer
This publication is designed to provide accurate and authoritative information in regard to the subject matter covered. It is sold with the understanding that the author and publisher are not engaged in rendering legal, accounting, or other professional services. If legal advice or other expert assistance is required, the services of a competent professional should be sought. The prophetic insights and business strategies shared are based on the author's personal experiences and spiritual journey; individual results in business may vary.

First Edition: February 2026
Paperback ISBN: 979-8-9947179-0-5
Ebook ISBN: 979-8-9947179-1-2

Published by *Cosmos Renewed Publishing*
Published in the United States of America
https://unknownsrising.com/

To K.J.S, J.K.S, and T.J.S.

You are the best treasure a man could hope for on this side of eternity.
Through every fiery trial, you believed in me when doubt whispered louder than
faith.
This book exists because you stood with me in the furnace and never let go.

Contents

Foreword by Roselyn Staples

IF YOU WERE INVITED to come look through a window to see what God is doing in our day, would you do it?

Art Serna, through the authorship of this book, extends this invitation.

As you read, you will find yourself in Art's personal story – welcomed as an observer of a prophetic vision, reminded of biblical foundations of faith, and made aware of the unique opportunities that our time in history is presenting to us.

I met Art and his family in 2020 when they became part of **World Impact Ministries** in Pewaukee, Wisconsin. The first time I heard him speak to our fellowship I knew this was a man to whom I wanted to listen. He spoke with confidence and power about who God is and what He is about to do in our time.

My spiritual story had not made room for prophetic revelation, so my intrigue was boundaried by caution. As a child of Norwegian immigrants, the Lutheran Church was my anchor. It was there that I fell deeply in love with Jesus. Adult life, in a different community, drew me to an Evangelical megachurch where I served as a pastor for 30 years. For the last ten years, I have worshiped with World Impact, a small charismatic fellowship with a vision of being a church "beyond the walls."

One of these "beyond the walls" outreach ministries involved connecting praying *Grandmas* with Art and his wife, Karen, at City on a Hill. It was in this context of watching these leaders, who would have been successful anywhere, pour out their lives for the forgotten and unseen that I was continually drawn to take a closer look at their lives and listen more intently to their teaching.

As I did, my caution regarding the prophetic transitioned from a flashing red light to an invitational green.

It was with high anticipation that I agreed to beta-read *The Unknowns Rising*. I was expecting to gain insights into the challenges of the next generation of Jesus followers. Having been born in the joint between the **Silent Generation** and the **Boomers**, the distance from **Gen Z** seemed long. I knew I needed help. What I was unprepared for was that, as I read, I was finding myself a patient in this story, undergoing explorative spiritual surgery.

I'll share two findings discovered by the surgical eyes of this book. *One is that I don't feel like I fit anywhere either.* As a youth I grew up with values more consistent with a Scandinavian culture than North American. As an adult follower of Jesus, I am not a poster child for any denomination. I am (not was) Lutheran, I am (not was) Evangelical, I am (not was) Charismatic. I might be becoming Apostolic/Prophetic. Thankfully, this book affirms me by teaching me that my in-between is not my disability but my superpower!

The second surgical finding is that I have been an integral part of church structures looking so unlike Jesus. I have long said that a relationship with God is our goal rather than the practice of religion. But as I read this book, I recognize that I have been hardwired by self-serving structures, cultural compromise, and practical advantage. I have done well in our cultural structures that support the inheritance of generational wealth. While it is true that my grandparents immigrated because of famine and clawed their way to a survival wage, the ladders we were given as European immigrants had rungs for climbing higher. I have deep friendships with people from other ethnic groups whose heritage provided two poles but no rungs to climb.

I rejoice that in the spiritual tenets of this book; God provides a ladder. **Genesis 28** gives us a picture of Jacob seeing a ladder between heaven and earth in a dream where God made a covenant with him and blessed his lineage. He does the same for the unknowns and His children.

I am eager for you to engage with the content of *this book*. As an appetizer, I am simply listing a few of the phrases that have stirred a hunger in me to be all that God has created me to be:

- *Can you see what God is doing, can you hear His call? Can you perceive the shift?*

- *The kingdom of God is breaking into the earth.*

- *Build, create and heal from the supernatural realm with the values of their Creator.*

- *Purification through encounter, not just information.*

- *Mentors see potential in the overlooked. The unknowns need your belief.*

- *The zeal of the Lord to heal a broken world.*

This book is not a "read-it-quickly" and put it on the shelf as a keepsake, but rather it is a companion that you read slowly and let become your trusted friend. I am remembering a conversation I had with my five-year old nephew when I was a children's pastor. My nephew said, "Aunty, I have figured out how to not get bored in Sunday School." Aware that I needed to listen closely to this insight I responded, "Tell me." He simply answered, "Put yourself in the story."

The Unknowns Rising invites you to put yourself in the story. I am excited for what you will learn about yourself, the God Who loves you and Who has designed you to be an intergenerational bridge.

The invitation to look through the window now leads you to walk over the threshold toward becoming who God designed you to be and do.

Welcome to *The Unknowns Rising*!

Roselyn Staples
January 2026

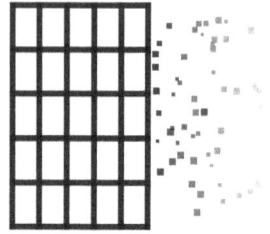

Introduction: The List Is Changing

THE MOMENT EVERYTHING SHIFTED

March 11, 2020: The World Stops

In March 2020, I was leading Teach For America in Oklahoma City. My family and I lived for the energy of the Thunder games, and that night, our staff sat in the stands as the starting lineups were announced. The arena was electric as the teams prepared for tip-off.

Then everything stopped.

After hurried discussions among officials, the teams returned to their locker rooms and the officials exited the court. The public address announcer informed the crowd the game had been postponed due to "unforeseen circumstances." Rudy Gobert had tested positive for coronavirus, and the NBA suspended its regular season. Teams were quarantined in the locker rooms and everyone was asked to go home.

The NBA didn't just postpone a game. They signaled the end of the world as we knew it. Within days, the streets went quiet, the schools locked their doors, and the global engine ground to a halt.

A Time of Reflection

From that moment, my family spent time in reflection, time in Scripture, and time in prayer. We continued to support our partners and everyone impacted as schools closed down, but something deeper was happening. The world slowed down and quieted, and I heard differently.

I felt a shift in my spirit. The world was resetting, and the constant noise of my career finally faded into the background. In that new silence, I didn't just hear my own thoughts. I heard God.

Joseph and Daniel

I thought about the stories of Joseph and Daniel in Scripture. Both went through challenging seasons where their lives were at risk, and both were thrust into environments foreign to their upbringing and comfort zones. They didn't choose these moments, but they prepared for them.

They spent time in prayer and reflection. Both had the ability to dream, interpret dreams, or see visions, and this revelatory insight became beneficial to the leaders of their time. Joseph interpreted Pharaoh's dream and saved the lives of his family and the Jewish people. Daniel interpreted the king's dream and saved the wise men from execution. Both had glimpses of the future before it arrived, and both acted on what they saw.

These two stories have meaning in my life because I've walked between worlds like they did. I've faced moments where everything familiar disappeared, and I've learned to listen when the noise stops. I've learned that God often speaks loudest in the disruptions, in the seasons when the old systems break down and new possibilities emerge.

Seven months later, in October 2020, I had a vision.

I saw a list with names I didn't recognize and faces from communities historically locked out of wealth creation. Inventors. Creators. Builders. I saw a new billionaire class rising from the edges of society. These leaders weren't coming from Manhattan boardrooms or Silicon Valley firms. They were rising from the very neighborhoods where we were always told to just be grateful for a steady paycheck.

The vision was clear: God was about to release a generation of unknowns. People dismissed by traditional gatekeepers. People told their dreams were too big. People who grew up translating for their parents, navigating multiple worlds, and solving problems no one else saw because no one else lived in the tension between cultures, languages, and economic realities.

The tools were ready, the barriers were falling, and the window was opening. But the window wouldn't stay open forever.

■ ■ ■

Why This Book Exists

I couldn't shake the vision.

October 2020. Three months after arriving in Milwaukee. Seven months after the world stopped. I saw names I didn't recognize and faces from places the Forbes list ignores, and the question haunted me: **What do you do when God shows you the future?**

I have two kids, and they're growing up in a world nothing like the one I inherited. The rules that governed my parents' generation are dissolving, the barriers that held back entire communities are crumbling, and the tools that once belonged only to the elite are now in everyone's hands. But knowing the future and preparing for it are two different things.

I kept thinking about the cupbearer in Joseph's story. He had a dream and Joseph interpreted it, but then the cupbearer forgot about Joseph for two years. Two years of Joseph sitting in prison, waiting. Then Pharaoh had a dream no one could interpret, and the cupbearer remembered. That memory changed everything because it positioned Joseph to save nations.

What if this vision wasn't just for me? What if it was for you?

This book exists because I believe we're standing at a threshold moment, a generational wealth transfer unlike anything in history. Not from old money to new money, but from no access to full access. Not from one elite class to another, but from locked doors to open windows. From communities told to stay in their lane to communities building entirely new roads.

Think about it: the wealthiest people in the world right now didn't inherit their fortunes from Rockefeller or Carnegie. They built them with technology, with platforms, with ideas that didn't exist a generation ago. Bezos didn't come from retail royalty. Musk didn't inherit an automotive empire. Zuckerberg didn't descend from media moguls. They saw a window and they moved.

Now that window is opening again, but this time it's opening for people who've been locked out for generations. People who look like you. People who sound like you. People who grew up translating at parent-teacher conferences and navigating systems designed to keep them out.

But windows don't stay open forever.

This book is my act of stewardship and my answer to the question: What is my obligation when God reveals what's coming?

This book is your invitation to step through the window while it's still open.

Who This Book Is For

If you're reading this, you are part of this shift.

You've moved between multiple worlds—cultural, linguistic, economic—and you've felt the tension between where you came from and where you're going. You've carried dreams that feel too big for your circumstances, and you've heard the voices (sometimes from people who love you) telling you to be realistic, to be grateful for what you have, to stop reaching for things that aren't meant for people like you.

You've been told, directly or indirectly, that wealth creation isn't for people like you. That you need to be grateful for stability. That dreaming too big is dangerous. That the billionaire class is reserved for people with the right last names, the right zip codes, the right access to capital and networks.

I'm here to tell you: *the rules have changed.*

The tools are available, the barriers are lower, and the window is open. But you need to move now. Not recklessly and not without wisdom, but with urgency. Not with the desperation of someone chasing money, but with the confidence of someone who knows they were made for this moment.

This window won't stay open forever. Technology will continue to democratize access, but it will also consolidate power. Early movers will gain advantages that compound over time. Networks will form and new gatekeepers will emerge. The difference between those who build generational wealth in the next decade and those who miss the opportunity will come down to one thing: whether they moved when the window was open.

The next five to ten years will determine who seizes this moment and who misses it.

■ ■ ■

My Journey to This Moment

I shouldn't be writing this book.

Born in the US but raised in Mexico from kindergarten through third grade, I returned to South Texas in fourth grade speaking better Spanish than English. I spent my childhood translating for my parents at doctor's appointments, parent-teacher conferences, in the spaces between two worlds. I was American by birth, Mexican by experience, and caught between two versions of what success was supposed to look like.

Small-town South Texas kid. Graduated valedictorian. Earned a scholarship to the University of Texas at Austin. Studied astronomy because I wanted to understand how the universe worked and added Latin American studies because I wanted to understand how I fit into it. I completed my undergrad in three and a half years with honors, and everyone expected me to take the corporate track, to climb the ladder, to secure the stability my parents had worked so hard to give me.

Then I did something unexpected.

I walked away from the ladder and into the work that mattered. Twenty-five years in the trenches of nonprofits, government agencies, education reform, and community health. United Way. Texas Child Protective Services. Charter school advocacy. Teach For America in Oklahoma City. A Milwaukee ministry where I discovered that the overlooked are the ones with the courage to change the world.

Those years taught me how systems actually work. How power moves. How resources get protected. And how decisions are made about who gets access and who gets left behind.

I watched families work three jobs and still fall behind. I saw brilliant minds boxed in by zip codes. I met entrepreneurs carrying million-dollar ideas with zero access to capital. I saw entire communities trained to be grateful for stability, while others, people with the right connections, the right networks, and the right last names, quietly built generational wealth.

Then I started noticing something else.

The old gatekeepers were losing their keys. AI started handing out expertise to anyone with a laptop, and 3D printing meant you could run a manufacturing line from your garage. You no longer needed a PhD or a factory to compete. No-code platforms were eliminating technical barriers so you didn't need to be a programmer to launch software. Online marketplaces were bypassing traditional gatekeepers so you didn't need retail distribution to reach customers. Crowdfunding was rewriting the rules of capital access so you didn't need venture capitalists to fund your vision.

The barriers that kept people out for generations were crumbling in real time, and I had spent 25 years learning how the old system worked. Now I was watching a new system emerge, one that didn't care about your last name, your zip code, or your access to legacy networks.

Then came October 2020.

The vision. The list. The names I didn't recognize. The faces from communities historically locked out. Everything I had seen, everything I had learned, and everything I had experienced moving between worlds, it all clicked.

This wasn't just about me. This was about all of us. This was about the mentors who see potential in the overlooked, the dreamers who refuse to accept the limitations others place on them, and the builders who are about to reshape the global economy. **And all of them share one thing in common:** *they prepare.*

The Prophetic Preparation Framework

You don't stumble into prophetic moments. You prepare for them.

Joseph didn't interpret Pharaoh's dream by accident. He spent years in prison developing character, managing Potiphar's household, and learning Egyptian systems. When the moment came, he was ready. Daniel didn't decode the king's vision on a whim. He spent years studying, praying, and building relationships with other wise men. When the crisis hit, he had the foundation to stand.

This is your **prophetic roadmap**, a framework for preparing for your moment:

1. Recognize the Season (Discernment)

You must learn to spot the shift. Watch the cracks in the old systems and look for the tools that are filling the gaps. Listen to the builders who are solving problems today that didn't even have a name five years ago. The world doesn't stop often, so when it does, listen. When industries collapse and new technologies emerge, when the rules change and the gatekeepers lose their grip, you're in a prophetic season.

2. Develop Your Skills (Preparation)

Joseph managed a household before managing a nation, and Daniel studied before interpreting. You need to build competence in your season of obscurity, in the years when no one is watching and no one believes in your vision except you and God. Learn the tools, master the platforms, and solve small problems before tackling big ones. Build the prototype before you pitch the vision. Serve the ten customers before you scale to ten thousand.

3. Cultivate Your Network (Positioning)

Both Joseph and Daniel had relationships that mattered when the moment came. The cupbearer remembered Joseph and the wise men stood with Daniel. Your network determines your access, so build relationships before you need them. Connect with other builders, other dreamers, other people who see what you see. Find mentors who've walked the path ahead of you and peers who are walking it beside you.

4. Stay Rooted in Faith (Foundation)

When everything shifts, your foundation matters. Joseph and Daniel prayed, stayed connected to God, and didn't compromise their values for shortcuts. They didn't abandon their faith when the pressure mounted, and they didn't trade their integrity for advancement. Your faith isn't decoration. It's your operating system. It's the lens through which you see opportunities, the compass that guides your decisions, and the anchor that holds you steady when everything around you is shifting.

5. Move When the Door Opens (Action)

Prophetic moments require decisive action. Joseph didn't hesitate when Pharaoh called and Daniel didn't delay when the king needed answers. When your moment comes, you move—not recklessly, but without hesitation. Not with arrogance, but with confidence. Not alone, but with the network you've built and the faith that sustains you.

This framework works for new generation leaders because you already live in disruption. You've watched institutions fail and seen technology reshape everything. You don't trust the old gatekeepers and you're looking for something real, something actionable, something that works. You're looking for a path that honors your faith without ignoring the practical realities of building wealth. You're looking for mentors who see potential in the overlooked, who understand that your bicultural experience isn't a liability but a superpower.

This is it.

What You Will Learn

In the chapters ahead, we'll explore:

- **The democratization of creation** and how technology has lowered the barriers to invention so you can build products, launch platforms, and solve problems without the resources that used to be required.

- **The fungible billionaire class** and why wealth creation is now a skill you can learn, not an inheritance you have to be born into.

- **The tools of transformation:** AI, 3D printing, online platforms, and more—the specific technologies you can use today to start building.

- **Your bicultural advantage is your greatest asset.** That 'in-between' feeling you've carried since childhood isn't a burden. It is the very perspective that allows you to see the gaps and opportunities that everyone else misses.

- **The path to monetization** and how to turn ideas into income, how to move from vision to prototype to revenue.

- **The prophetic call** and how to step into your destiny as a creator, as someone who doesn't just consume what others build but builds what others need.

This is not theory. This is practical, actionable, and tested. I will share my journey, the lessons I learned, the mistakes I made, the tools I use, the networks I built, and the faith that sustains me. I will show you how to blend purpose with profit, how to build something bigger than yourself, and how to solve meaningful problems while creating sustainable wealth.

I will show you how Joseph's story and Daniel's story connect to your story, how ancient wisdom applies to modern technology, and how faith becomes the operating system for building generational wealth.

The Promise

By the end of this book, you will have:

- **A clear understanding** of the economic shift happening right now and why this moment is different from anything your parents or grandparents experienced.

- **A toolkit of accessible technologies** you can use today, with specific examples of how people like you are already using them to build wealth.

- **A framework for identifying problems** worth solving, problems that people will pay you to solve because they're real and urgent and valuable.

- **A strategy for building networks** that amplify your impact, networks that connect you to mentors, collaborators, and customers.

- **A prophetic roadmap** for turning your vision into reality, a step-by-step process for moving from idea to execution to scale.

Most importantly, you will have permission.

Permission to dream bigger than your circumstances. Permission to create wealth in ways your parents never imagined. Permission to step into your calling as one of the unknowns rising. Permission to believe that God didn't give you this vision just to watch you ignore it.

We often hide behind a comfortable faith. We pick the scriptures that promise stability and ignore the ones that demand risk. We've been trained to stay in our lane, but God is calling you to pave a new one. We've been taught to be grateful for stability, to accept our limitations, to stay in our lane.

But what if God is calling you to build a new lane? What if the vision He gave you requires you to risk the limitless resources of God rather than weigh your access to your own emotional and financial resources?

■ ■ ■

Before We Go Further

Pause. Close your eyes. Take a deep breath.

Ask yourself: Do I believe the future is different than the past?

Not for "people out there." For you. For your family. For your community.

If the answer is yes—even a tentative, uncertain yes—keep reading. The window is open. The tools are ready. Your name is on the list.

You were born for such a time as this.

The Vision

WHEN HEAVEN INVADES EARTH

> In the year that King Uzziah died, I saw the Lord, high and exalted, seated on a throne; and the train of his robe filled the temple. Above him were seraphim, each with six wings: With two wings they covered their faces, with two they covered their feet, and with two they were flying. And they were calling to one another: "Holy, holy, holy is the Lord Almighty; the whole earth is full of his glory." At the sound of their voices the doorposts and thresholds shook and the temple was filled with smoke.
>
> Isaiah 6:1–4, NIV

OCTOBER 2020. PEWAUKEE, WISCONSIN.

Worship had carried us for twenty minutes. Voices rose, hands reached, and the very air in the room grew heavy with a hunger for God. I wasn't a speaker that night.

I wasn't a leader on the platform. I was a stranger in a new city, only three months into my Milwaukee journey, kneeling in the quiet of the crowd.

I was nearing the end of a season of prayer and fasting, seeking God's face for my community as we emerged from the global pandemic. I was positioning myself to align with what He was doing in Milwaukee, in the nation, and in my own heart.

Music has always done something to me. King David used music to connect to the deep parts of his heart and with the heart of God, and music refines my ear, my ability to hear, to see, and to receive revelation beyond the normal. As the songs continued, the atmosphere shifted and it was not just worship anymore. It was an invitation. A doorway opening.

I felt it before I saw it.

The Encounter

My knees were on the floor, my eyes were closed, and my heart was open.

Then it came.

The weight hit me. It wasn't a sound, yet it was louder than the music. It wasn't a physical sight, yet it burned brighter than the lights in the room. I call it a download because the information bypassed my brain and went straight to my spirit. I didn't just see a list; I recognized a new reality.

I looked, and a vision was set before me. It was the list of the world's wealthiest, the names that have anchored global power for a generation. Bezos. Musk. Gates. Buffett. Zuckerberg. The names were static, fixed in their positions like monuments of the past.

Then the list began to shift.

■ ■ ■

The Shifting List

Number seven moved to number three. Number three moved to number one. Number 10 disappeared and a new name appeared.

The names on the screen began to fracture and reform. This wasn't a slow transition; it was a violent disruption. The old guard, the names that had anchored the Forbes list for decades, began to slide. In their place rose names the world didn't recognize. Names from the margins. **Names of the unknowns.** God was rewriting the ledger of global influence in real time.

A truth settled into my spirit: the list of billionaires was no longer a monument. It was becoming fluid. The era of the static elite, the same five names occupying the top for twenty years, was over. The ledger was shifting with a violent speed, but the movement of the names was only the beginning. There was something deeper happening beneath the surface.

Some of the names appearing on the list were people from poverty, from distressed backgrounds, from generational struggle. The words from **Psalm 113** hit me like a ton of bricks:

> Who is like the LORD our God, the One who sits enthroned on high, who stoops down to look on the heavens and the earth? He raises the poor from the dust and lifts the needy from the ash heap; he seats them with princes, with the princes of his people.
>
> Psalm 113:5-8, NIV

I was leading a ministry in Milwaukee focused on loving and serving those with generational poverty, people society had written off, people from the "wrong" backgrounds. In the vision, some of those types of individuals were landing on the billionaire list.

Not in 50 years. Not in some distant future. Soon. Through the season of change, but soon.

There was a shift of power, peace, perspective, and influence happening before my eyes.

Economic systems would begin to change in dramatic ways. Century-level change. It was coming. It was already upon us.

And these that would arise would be different. They would blend spiritual wisdom, divine revelation, and cutting-edge technology. A new type of science. New tech and physics applied to creative design, and their emergence would mean mass destruction to the systems of darkness that oppress humanity and devastate the earth.

The sense was clear: "This is done. This is imminent. This will happen. Get ready for it."

That was the urgency I felt, and it has not left me since.

■ ■ ■

The Synergy of the Self

In that moment, there was more.

An understanding. An awareness of the fullness of humanity. The makeup of mankind: body, soul, spirit. Fully leveraging the Creator's code written into DNA and the divine design embedded in human biology to thrust God's kingdom blueprint forward. This would be a key part of the shift.

Individuals would come into a growing awareness of wholeness, identity, purpose, and completeness. Understanding the full makeup from their Creator and how to function within it. No longer would people live in siloed, fractured, separated, isolated lives, even within themselves. Instead, they would come into a synergy of the self, coming together and becoming whole.

This wholeness ignites a new level of creation. When a man stops fighting himself, he starts solving problems for the world. Courage ceases to be an effort and becomes a reflex. These leaders won't just 'think outside the box'; they will build entirely new worlds because they are operating from a completed soul.

This was connected to inventions, new scientists, scientific advancements, and philosophies of knowing. Peace in it all. I saw the list changing and people would be shocked. "How did this happen? How did this name, this individual, make it on here? Who is this person?"

And they would not be defined as representing *socialism* or *communism* or *capitalism*. **It would be a new breed altogether, operating from a different set of values and a different source of power.**

The David Archetype

Much in the likeness of King David.

Deemed the least of his brothers, out of nowhere he came on the scene and the Prophet Samuel anointed him. Samuel was looking at the sons of Jesse for the physical aesthetics of a king, but then he realized something profound:

> The Lord does not look at the things people look at. People look
> at the outward appearance, but the Lord looks at the heart.
> 1 Samuel 16:7, NIV

This was the concept. This evolution. This change.

It would not be like before. It would be as if God Himself were selecting, advancing, and raising up the unknowns, and as they achieved the list, they would not have a self-seeking attitude or perspective. This was change benefiting humanity.

These billionaires carry a different DNA. They possess an empathy forged in the fire of rejection. Because they grew up far from the tables of power, they understand the weight of a need in a way a trust-fund heir never could. They didn't just study poverty; they outlived it. Now, they are rising to solve it.

But now, they were rising.

This is the question you might be asking: *How do we know that the new generation of wealth holders won't be selfish wrongdoers too?*

Here's what I perceived: there would be a transformative work in them prior to and accompanying the transition. **Like David,** they would be anointed before they were crowned. **Like Joseph**, they would be refined in the prison before they were elevated to the palace. **Like Daniel**, they would prove their character in obscurity before they were trusted with influence.

The wealth would not corrupt them because the wealth would not define them. Their identity would be rooted in God, and their purpose would be rooted in service. They would carry the empathy of those who have suffered and the wisdom of those who have been refined by fire.

The Unknowns and Their Guides

The vision holds significance for two groups.

The unknowns. Those carrying dreams too big for their current circumstances. Those navigating multiple worlds. Those told (directly or indirectly) wealth creation is not for people like them.

The mentors. Those who have already walked through fire. Those who built something from nothing. Those who know the cost of the journey and refuse to let the next generation walk it alone.

Both are essential and both are part of this shift.

If you are an unknown, hear me: *your obscurity is not a prison.* It is your protection. God is refining you in the shadows so you don't break in the light. The world doesn't know your name yet, but the Father has already written it on the list. Your job isn't to chase fame; your job is to master the tools He has placed in your hands.

If you are a mentor, you need to understand something: *your greatest contribution is not your success.* Your greatest contribution is your willingness to see potential in people others overlook, to invest in the unlikely, to open doors you had to break down, and to pass on wisdom that cost you everything to learn.

The unknowns need you. Not your money. Not your connections. Your belief.

The Promise and the Problem

> Jesus looked at them and said, "With man this is impossible, but with God all things are possible."
>
> Matthew 19:26, NIV

This is the promise.

The unknowns are rising. The billionaire class is shifting. Technology is democratizing wealth creation. God is calling the overlooked, the border-crossers, the bicultural, the Gen Z, the Latinos, the "wrong background" people.

With man, this is impossible. People like us do not become billionaires. We do not create world-changing inventions. We do not sit at tables of power and influence.

But with God, all things are possible to those who believe.

This is the promise I received in October 2020, but there is a problem as old as Isaiah's time. Most people cannot see this. They are *"ever seeing but never perceiving"* (Isaiah 6:9), and you can look directly at the future and miss it entirely.

They see the Forbes list. They see the same names. They see the barriers. They see their own limitations.

But they do not perceive the shift happening underneath. They do not perceive the tools appearing. They do not perceive God's hand moving.

Your job, my job, is to help them see. To open eyes. To unstop ears. To help people perceive what God is doing right now.

■ ■ ■

The Abrahamic Call

My move to Milwaukee was an Abrahamic departure.

I didn't just leave Texas; I severed my connection to the comfort of family gatherings and the familiar rhythms of home. I stepped into the unknown, traveling toward a place where God would establish a promise. This wasn't just for me. It was for my children, and for generations I will never meet.

My mother calls me "*Estrellita*". Little star. She spoke a prophetic truth over me before I understood the cost. To shine brightly often requires distance. To be a star in God's kingdom, I had to be willing to shine in a different sky.

This is the cost of the prophetic call. Abraham left his people. Moses left Egypt. David left the sheep. Paul left his reputation. The call always requires leaving something behind, but the promise is always greater than the sacrifice.

The vision I received in Milwaukee was not just about me. It was about a generation, a movement, and a shift in how wealth is created, who creates it, and what it is used for.

This book is my obedience to that call, but this is not just my story. This is your invitation.

The window of opportunity is open right now. Technologies that once required billions in capital are available to anyone with vision and internet access. The barriers have fallen and the gatekeepers have lost their power.

The question is no longer whether you have access. The question is whether you will step through the door.

■ ■ ■

The Dread and the Awe

I was still kneeling. The worship was still going. People around me were praying, singing, and encountering God in their own ways.

But I was undone.

Isaiah saw the Lord, high and exalted, and the train of His robe filled the temple. Seraphim cried, "Holy, holy, holy," and the doorposts shook. Isaiah's response?

> "Woe to me! I am ruined! For I am a man of unclean lips, and I live among a people of unclean lips, and my eyes have seen the King, the Lord Almighty."
>
> Isaiah 6:5, NIV

I felt the same. Dread. Awe. Unworthiness.

Who was I to receive this vision? A South Texas kid. First-generation college graduate. No deep tech background. No billions. No compelling platform. Not a mainstream prophet.

I was leading a small ministry in Milwaukee. I was new to this church. I was nobody, yet I had seen something. Something massive. Something that felt like it came from outside of time.

I felt like David showing up at the Jewish camp as they were mocked by Goliath. Internally, I had peace that God was wooing me closer and choosing to release His revelation to me as to a friend. But externally, I felt inadequate, awkward, and out of place.

Yet God was there. His voice validating. A paradox.

But I Was Not Ready

Isaiah saw the Lord. He cried out, "Woe to me! I am ruined!" I had the same response internally. I was not ready for this vision. I was not worthy. I was ruined.

I had unclean lips. I lived among a people of unclean lips. I was a man of the border. A man between worlds. A man who had failed. A man who had limitations.

Who was I to carry this message? Who was I to help the unknowns rise? I would soon find out.

The vision was only the invitation. The purification was the price. I felt the heat of the altar before I felt the weight of the call. The coal was coming for my lips, and I knew one thing for certain: it was going to burn.

■ ■ ■

Reflection Questions

1. **Have you ever had a moment** when you felt God was showing you something about the future? How did you respond?

2. **What "impossibilities" in your life** might become possible if you truly believed Matthew 19:26?

3. **Who are the "unknowns"** in your community who are rising? How can you support them?

4. **What would it look like** for you to move with urgency in this season? What is one step you can take this week?

5. **Do you feel "ready"** for what God is calling you to? Why or why not?

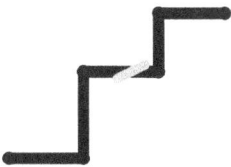

The Struggle to Believe

RECOGNIZING YOUR INADEQUACY

"Woe to me!" I cried. "I am ruined! For I am a man of unclean lips, and I live among a people of unclean lips, and my eyes have seen the King, the Lord Almighty."

Isaiah 6:5, NIV

ISAIAH SAW THE LORD, high and exalted, and the train of His robe filled the temple. Seraphim cried, *"Holy, holy, holy,"* and his response was not joy but terror. *"Woe to me! I am ruined!"* In the presence of holiness, Isaiah saw his sin clearly, his unworthiness, and his inadequacy to carry the message God was about to give him. He saw that his words had been shaped by a broken world, that he spoke from a place of woundedness, and that he lived among people who were equally wounded.

I felt the same in October 2020, kneeling on the floor in Pewaukee, Wisconsin, with the vision still fresh and the billionaire list shifting before my eyes. **Who was I to receive this vision?** I spoke from woundedness, and I lived among the wounded, and yet God had chosen me to see something that would change everything.

Before I tell you about the wounds, I need to tell you about the truth, because the truth is what makes the wounds matter.

In September 2018, while leading in Oklahoma City, I felt the pull of a desert season. I drove south to Texas for a men's retreat, desperate for clarity and a direct word from God. During the session, we engaged in a prophetic exercise of renaming—mirroring the moment Jesus transformed Simon into Peter. As the men prayed over me, a single word cut through the noise and anchored my soul: *Imager*. They didn't just choose a title; they recognized the identity the Father had already written into my spirit.

You are an ***imager*** of the Creator. Your Creator. That is who you are was the resounding message.

This wasn't just a new name; it was a reclamation of my DNA. To be an **Imager** means I carry the raw *creative frequency* of the God of Abraham. I don't just 'reflect' His virtues, I am hardwired to manifest them. Excellence isn't an ideal I'm chasing; it is the code written into my very soul. I was built to build.

For me, the vastness of the cosmos serves as a divine summons, a call to be a faithful steward of the resources we have been entrusted with. This is our mandate: to take what is given and leave it better than we found it. While I often fall short of this ideal, the drive to cultivate excellence is woven into my very DNA. It is a truth that resonates in my spirit. I am on the journey of an 'imager,' a visionary called to create beauty and value that not only enriches my own experience but leaves a lasting legacy for my family and the world.

This is the foundational truth: I am an imager. Fashioned in the very likeness of God, I am called to create, called to build, and called to reflect His transcendent glory. Yet, by October 2020, two years after that transformative retreat, the distance between my calling and my reality felt insurmountable. I did not feel like an imager. Instead, I felt like an imposter, struggling to find my footing in the most vital areas of my life.

■ ■ ■

Who Was I?

My spirit was willing, but my flesh argued against the call. Those arguments were loud, and they were convincing. I questioned what could possibly qualify me to receive such a vision. I was a kid from South Texas, born in McAllen and raised in Reynosa, Mexico. I moved to the United States in the fourth grade, eventually becoming the first in my family to graduate from college. Even with that milestone, I had no background in deep tech, no billions in the bank, and no platform.

I felt like a nobody who lived among people who did not believe this level of success was possible for us. In our world, people from small beginnings do not become billionaires. We do not create world-changing inventions, and we do not sit at tables of power. We are taught to be grateful for stability. We work hard, and we provide for our families, but we do not dream too big.

I had internalized these limits without knowing it, and I carried them like a heavy weight. The truth was that I am an imager, but the lie told me I was disqualified. My flesh relied on worldly arguments of self-validation, upbringing, and belonging. These arguments were not just personal. They were cultural, systemic, and generational. They were lies built upon lies, compounded over lifetimes and set in motion through bloodlines long before I arrived on the scene.

The Bicultural Wound

I have lived my life in the tension of the 'in-between.' In Mexico, I was a stranger; in America, I was an exile. This 'bicultural wound' isn't just a feeling, it is a systemic argument designed to breed a philosophy of lack. It whispers that you are never enough for either world. But I had to learn that my exile wasn't a mistake; it was my training ground. Like Daniel in Babylon, I was being taught to master a foreign system without losing my soul.

My foundation was poured in Reynosa, Mexico. From kindergarten through third grade, my world was defined by crisp uniforms, the rhythmic pride of the Mexican national anthem, and the exclusive cadence of Spanish. My parents were relentless, grinding to break into the middle class, which often left my brothers and me as latchkey kids, claiming the streets as our Playground. Though Val and I held U.S. citizenship by birth, my younger brother, Frank, was born in Reynosa, a legal distinction that would take him years to resolve. Despite my American birthright, Mexico owned my heart. Spanish was my tongue; Mexican culture was my soul.

The schools in Reynosa were forged in scarcity. We endured winters without heat and summers in classrooms where the windows refused to close, yet the lack of resources never dampened the mandate: education was our only bridge to a different life. My parents were pioneers, entrepreneurs who hadn't yet found their platform. My father labored as a handyman, a truck driver, and a butcher before rising to become a chef at the Hilton, commanding banquets for five hundred people. My mother balanced a cashier's drawer with the pursuit of her beautician certification in Texas. They didn't just work; they sacrificed. Like Jacob investing in Joseph, they were sowing into a future they would never inhabit. Like the parents of Daniel, they anchored us in excellence and the honor of God, even when the ground beneath us was shifting.

Life changed after third grade. My father secured a steady job with benefits at the Hilton in South Texas, and that position opened a new door for our family. My parents rented a house in McAllen, and we enrolled in the American education system. I still remember my first day at Sam Houston Elementary. My fourth-grade teacher, Ms. Gonzalez, was kind and patient. I needed her grace because I was suddenly learning fractions in a foreign system and navigating life in a bilingual program.

The culture shock was overwhelming. I was in my birth country, yet I did not understand the world around me. At home, we spoke Spanish, but at school, the references and jokes were entirely different. I struggled to fit in and felt the constant, heavy pressure to evolve into someone new. This was my exile moment. Like Joseph being sold into Egypt or Daniel being carried to Babylon, I was thrust into a foreign system. I had to learn a new language and navigate cultural expectations that were not designed for someone like me. I was surviving in the tension of the "in-between."

The Struggle to Belong

Our journey continued at Roosevelt Elementary, where we stayed for part of a semester. This period was markedly more difficult. My teacher was not bilingual, and the grace I had found with Ms. Gonzalez was gone. I felt less understood and less appreciated. Every day was a minefield of awkward cultural references and linguistic stumbles. I remember struggling to say something as simple as "Have a happy day." I stood there, staring at a plastic cup with a yellow smiley face, but the words died in my throat. 'Ave Appy Dai.' The syllables felt like stones in my mouth. I couldn't find the rhythm of this new world. In that moment, I wasn't just a student failing a language; I was a stranger realizing the world wasn't built for my voice.

Eventually, our family found stability. Through assistance programs, my parents purchased their first home in the Pharr-Hidalgo area, and we enrolled in Valley View Elementary. Val and I were initially placed in a bilingual classroom, but the trajectory of my life shifted when I was suddenly pulled out. I was moved into a full-immersion English program. Midway through the semester, Val was also moved up a grade to join me.

While this immersion accelerated our mastery of the language and placed us among the top students in our graduating class, it also deepened the bicultural wound. I was no longer fully Mexican, yet I was not fully American. I was caught in a cultural purgatory. To the Americans, I was too Mexican. To the Mexicans, I was too American. This is the weight of the "in-between." It is a life of constant translation and perpetual code-switching. It is the persistent, quiet hum of internalized shame.

This shame was reinforced by a chorus of voices from certain teachers, counselors, and the society around us. They spoke a limiting philosophy into our lives out of their own wounding: "People like us do not become billionaires. We do not create world-changing inventions. We should simply be grateful for stability."

This was the message I internalized deep down. It was the idea that we could work hard and provide for our families, but we must never dream too big. That kind of success was reserved for someone else. This cultural narrative plays on personal brokenness to create generational cycles of trauma. It becomes a distorted lens through which we view our own potential. When that lens is cracked, you cannot see clearly. You cannot see that you are, and have always been, an imager.

The Imposter Syndrome

The bicultural wound manifests as a specific, haunting shadow: imposter syndrome. Even as you achieve goals and receive recognition, a persistent voice whispers that you are a fraud. You feel as though you are merely acting a part, waiting for the moment someone realizes you do not belong. For years, this wound powered a hamster wheel of achievement. I sought external validation to silence internal insecurity.

This distortion even touched my natural design. When I eventually took the CliftonStrengths assessment, my top five themes emerged: Learner, Achiever, Futuristic, Strategic, and Self-Assurance. These are God-given talents, yet in 2020, I viewed them only through the lens of my wound. I believed I was a Learner because I was inadequate. I was an Achiever because I had to prove my worth. I was Futuristic because I hated my present. I was Strategic only because I felt I had to bypass systems that were not built for me. I was Self-Assured because I felt I had no one else to rely on.

What the enemy intended for my destruction, however, God began to redeem as humility. This syndrome kept me teachable and dependent on Him. To find healing, I first had to name the wound and recognize the lie.

The Theater Moment

My first true encounter with this "acting" happened in high school. On a Wednesday afternoon during my junior year, I was pulled from art class. The theater sponsor needed to speak with me. The school was producing Macbeth for a regional competition. I had a minor, insignificant role with a single line, and I only joined the cast because my friends were involved. I had no idea I possessed any creative ability.

The news was dire. The senior playing Macbeth had dropped out just days before the Saturday competition. The entire production was at risk of disqualification. They asked me to take the lead. Despite my status as a student-athlete and top-tier student, I doubted I could carry the weight of Shakespeare's most complex tragic hero.

With the principal's permission, I spent my days in isolation, running repetitions and diving into the mind of Macbeth. I stayed up through the nights, memorizing the rhythm of the lines and the descent of the character. By the time we arrived at the competition, the experience was a blur of adrenaline. We were competing against schools with massive budgets and elite departments. When the final curtain closed and I fell to the ground in Macbeth's death scene, I was simply grateful we had finished.

I was stunned when they called the awards. I sat in the audience as they announced my name for *Honorable Mention*. I held that medal with a sense of pure exhilaration.

The following year, we performed Ordinary People. I was cast as Dr. Berger, a psychiatrist. I stepped into the skin of Dr. Berger. Theater didn't just teach me to act; it forced me to develop the eyes of a seer. It demanded empathy, intuition, and the courage to stand in a reality that wasn't yet my own. God was using a high school stage to train me for a global vision. He was teaching me to interpret the unseen before He ever asked me to lead the unknowns.

At the end of the competition, as they reached the final two awards of the day, I felt a familiar sense of disappointment. I assumed I had been overlooked this time around.

Then, they called my name. **Arturo Serna. 3A Best Actor.**

I nearly fell out of my chair. I floated toward the stage to receive the award. To this day, it remains one of the most significant accomplishments of my life. Theater taught me to see through different eyes. It forced me to connect with emotion, intuition, and empathy. It revealed that curiosity and creativity are the keys to prophetic insight.

God was preparing me in the shadows, just as He prepared Joseph through dreams and Daniel through visions. He was teaching me to interpret what others could not see and to step into roles for which I felt unqualified. Yet, even then, the lens of the wound remained. I walked off that stage feeling that I was still just an actor. I still felt like I did not truly belong.

The Bicultural Advantage

Here lies the paradox: your bicultural wound is also your bicultural advantage. The pain of never fully belonging is the gift of seeing both worlds with clarity. The shame of being "too Mexican" or "too American" is the very strength required to bridge cultures. The struggle of code-switching is the skill of translating between kingdoms. Even the imposter syndrome serves a purpose; it is the humility that keeps you dependent on God. What the enemy intended for evil, God redeems as teachability.

As I drew closer to God and engaged in the Great Commission, I began to appreciate the strategic value of my upbringing. I could speak to multiple audiences and see patterns others missed. This was not a limitation. It was a gateway to becoming a vessel for the Most High. Joseph could interpret the dreams of Egypt because he understood both his Hebrew roots and the Egyptian court. Daniel could navigate Babylon because he was grounded in Jerusalem. Their bicultural experience was not a wound to be covered but a weapon to be wielded.

However, in October 2020, I did not yet see this truth. I was kneeling on the floor, crying out with the prophet Isaiah, *"Woe to me! I am ruined!"* I only saw my inadequacy and my fear of failure. That was exactly where God wanted me.

The Battle for the Mind

Becoming who God has called you to be is a spiritual battle. As the Apostle Paul writes:

> "We demolish arguments and every pretension that sets itself up against the knowledge of God, and we take captive every thought to make it obedient to Christ."
>
> 2 Corinthians 10:5, NIV

The bicultural wound is a lie masquerading as a fact. It is a generational pretension that claims you are disqualified by your zip code or your accent. We don't just 'name' these lies; we demolish them. We take every thought captive and force it to bow to the truth of our calling. If you believe your wound is greater than your mandate, you are insulting the Creator who fashioned you. The blood of Christ didn't just save your soul; it redeemed your potential. This must move from a concept in your mind to a revelation in your heart.

The Principle: Clear Sight Before Divine Service

Isaiah saw the Lord, but he also saw his own sin. He recognized his wounded perspective in the presence of transcendent majesty. This is the first step of the prophetic commission. Before God can use you, you must see yourself clearly. You must see your inadequacy in the flesh, your brokenness and your limitations, while simultaneously seeing your identity in Christ. Both are true. In the flesh, I am inadequate. In Christ, I am an imager.

This is the paradox of the Gospel. We are broken, yet being made whole. We are wounded, yet being healed. You cannot carry a prophetic message if you believe you are worthy on your own. You cannot help the "unknowns" rise if you think you have already arrived. You must see your imposter syndrome and your shame clearly, for only then can God purify you to represent Him as He truly is.

The Necessity of Purification

After Isaiah confessed his inadequacy, a seraph flew to him with a live coal taken from the altar. The angel touched Isaiah's mouth and said, "*See, this has touched your lips; your guilt is taken away and your sin atoned for.*"

Purification is never painless. I cried out for the vision, but I wasn't ready for the fire. I needed the coal to touch the very lips that had stuttered in that fourth-grade classroom. I didn't know then that the flame would lead me through a valley of total devastation. But the coal was coming.

And it was time to burn.

■ ■ ■

Reflection Questions

1. **What does it mean to you that you are an "imager" of God?** How does this truth challenge the way you currently see yourself?

2. **What cultural messages have shaped how you see yourself?** What have you been told (directly or indirectly) about "people like you"?

3. **How have you seen your God-given strengths through the lens of the wound?** (Example: "I'm a learner because I don't know enough" instead of "I'm a learner because God designed me to love growth.")

4. **What arguments and pretensions have set themselves up against the knowledge of God in your life?** What lies need to be demolished?

5. **Can you honestly say, "I am inadequate on my own, but chosen by God"?** What would it look like to see your inadequacy clearly before God without shame or self-hatred?

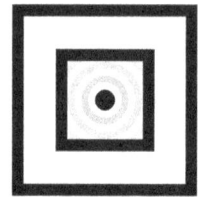

The Coal from the Altar — Part 1

PURIFICATION THROUGH ENCOUNTER

"Then one of the seraphim flew to me with a live coal in his hand, which he had taken with tongs from the altar. With it he touched my mouth and said, 'See, this has touched your lips; your guilt is taken away and your sin atoned for.'"

Isaiah 6:6–7, NIV

PURIFICATION STARTS IN FIRE. Not information. Not education. Not self-improvement. It starts when God meets you. Before I could steward anything, before I could build anything, God had to refine me with a heat I could not produce and a holiness I could not fake.

The Supernatural Inheritance

My journey into the fire did not start with me. It started with my maternal grandfather. He worked the ranches of South Texas through the Bracero program, and for years alcohol tried to take him out. Then God interrupted him through the Catholic faith, and that encounter did not just change a man. It changed our bloodline.

I heard the stories later. My grandmother described a man who served his community like he was on assignment. He opened homes for worship across Mexico, and he carried the presence of the Holy Spirit with him. He never became fully literate, yet he memorized Scripture by hearing my grandmother read it out loud. People told me he laid hands on priests and they fell, not from emotion, but from the weight of God.

He was an "unknown". No platform. No credentials. No formal education. Still, he carried a real spiritual inheritance, and it did not die with him. He was the first in our line to yield to the Spirit and live like the invisible world was more real than the visible one. He left a deposit, and one day God made it clear that I could not admire it from a distance. I had to claim it.

The Desperation of the First-Gen Student

By the time I reached the University of Texas, I was hungry for God. During my sophomore year, a speaker from Harvest Evangelism shared stories of the revival in Argentina. Something in those stories anchored into the legacy my grandfather had left behind. I knew I had to go.

I had no money for an international mission trip. I was first-generation, and my parents could not cover it. Neither could I. When the deadline hit, I locked myself in my parents' bathroom, sat on the floor, and cried silently until I ran out of words. I told God I did not need comfort. I needed a way.

In that moment of total surrender, the phone rang. A donor had provided the exact funding needed for the team. That was my first lesson in the Kingdom's economy. When God gives the assignment, surrender opens the door, and provision shows up on time.

The Argentine Encounter

In Buenos Aires, my bicultural background moved from a "wound" to a "weapon." Because I was bilingual, I was thrust into the center of the revival as a translator for generals of the faith. I saw business leaders crying out for their nation and saw churches unite in a way that defied logic.

One afternoon, traveling between ministry sites, heat settled on my chest like a hand. The weight pressed from within and from without, and I froze because I did not want to lose it. I whispered, *"Holy Spirit, do not leave me."* Right there I learned something I have never forgotten: His presence carries you past your personality. It carries you past your speed. He was strengthening my human limitations for an assignment I could not yet name.

The Double Portion

The turning point came in a conference room with Sergio Scataglini, an Argentine pastor who had authored *The Fire of His Holiness*. The atmosphere was thick with the fear of the Lord. Sergio had encountered God's holiness so intensely that it had nearly cost him his life.

When he finished speaking, something leapt inside me. I felt the same boldness that Elisha felt when he followed Elijah. I walked to the front, looked Sergio in the eye, and said in Spanish: *"I feel God told me to ask for a double portion of what you received."*

Sergio stopped. He looked at me with fire in his eyes and told me to wait. After praying for others, he returned with his associates. He warned me that what I was about to receive would change me forever, but it would come with a cost. He laid hands on me, and I fell under the power of God. I knew God had set me apart. Something was planted in me that would touch business and technology, but first it had to die in the dark. Refinement would bury it before it ever bore fruit.

■ ■ ■

The Pattern of Joseph and Daniel

Joseph and Daniel prove a pattern you cannot escape. Encounter lights the fire, and testing keeps it burning.

- **Joseph's Internal Fire:** Before Joseph stood in the palace, he was given dreams. Those dreams were a fire in his soul that his brothers could not understand. Like the coal in Isaiah, those dreams purified his motives through the pit and the prison. He had to be stripped of his "technicolor coat" of favor before he could be trusted with the "signet ring" of the steward.

- **Daniel's External Fire:** Daniel lived in the tension of two worlds. He was trained in the wisdom of Babylon but sustained by the visions of Jerusalem. His companions were literally thrown into a furnace, only to find that the fire did not consume them; it only burned their ropes.

This is the case for the unknowns. God is raising up a generation that does not rely on pedigree or platforms. He is raising up those who have been marked by the coal. Like Joseph, you may be in a season of "obscurity and fire." Like Daniel, you may be navigating a system that feels foreign. The fire is not there to destroy you. The fire burns the ego out of you so that when you sit at the table of influence, you represent the King, not yourself.

The Necessity of the Burn

Purification is not comfortable. Fire burns. God gave me my grandfather's legacy, the Argentine revival, and the "double portion" prayer, but these were not meant for my comfort. They were meant for my preparation.

If you are a member of Gen Z or a "next-gen" leader, understand this: your first fire encounter is just the beginning. It is the invitation to the journey. And if you are a mentor, your role is to see the "coal-marked" potential in those whom the world overlooks. You are not in the final chapter of your journey; you are the steward of the flame, called to pass the fire to the next generation of unknowns.

■ ■ ■

The Supernatural Advantage in an AI-First World

This is why the journey matters. You learn to fellowship with God until your cravings fall into order under His holiness. Validation loses its grip, comparison stops driving you, and your soul stops begging the world to tell you who you are. That death is slow, and it costs you more than you want to pay, but it makes you free.

And we need that freedom now. We live in a world where AI reshapes decisions, money, access, and influence. Systems move faster than most people can track, and new gatekeepers rise the moment the old ones fall. If you rely on credentials alone, you will miss what God is doing. If you rely on logic alone, you will misread the moment.

We need discernment like Joseph in Egypt, and we need courage like Daniel in Babylon. We need people who can stand inside powerful systems without bowing to them. My grandfather learned that in the fields of South Texas. I tasted it in Argentina. I learned it again on that bus when the Holy Spirit settled on me with weight. The fire of God does not just comfort you. It rebuilds you. It trains you to lead through pressure without losing your soul.

We are not qualified by pedigree. We are not qualified by platforms. We are qualified by encounter, and then we are proven in the fire.

The Coal Was Not Finished

The seraph touched Isaiah's lips with the coal from the altar and declared that his guilt was taken away and his sin atoned for. Isaiah's coal did its work in a moment. Mine did not. Argentina marked me, but it did not finish me. Now God would shape me through heat, silence, and trial.

■ ■ ■

Reflection Questions

1. **Identify your spiritual inheritance.** Who in your family line walked in the fire before you? If you are the first to encounter God in this way, what legacy are you now commissioned to build for the generations to follow?

2. **Recall your "burning bush" or "bus ride" moment.** Describe the time you experienced the tangible presence of the Holy Spirit. How did that encounter redefine your identity as an "imager" rather than just a worker?

3. **Evaluate the cost of the fire.** Every encounter with God's holiness requires a surrender of the flesh. What did your previous encounters cost you, and what is the specific "comfort" God is asking you to release today?

4. **Consider the "double portion."** Are you willing to ask for a prophetic anointing that exceeds your current capacity, knowing it will require a deeper level of death to self? What is the cost you are most afraid to pay?

5. **Examine your internal arguments.** In this era of rapid AI development and shifting systems, where do you still rely on your own logic or credentials? What roots of pride or self-assurance must be uprooted to make room for supernatural fellowship?

6. **Bridge the two worlds.** Like Joseph and Daniel, how is your unique background or "bicultural wound" currently being retooled by the Spirit into a prophetic advantage for the marketplace?

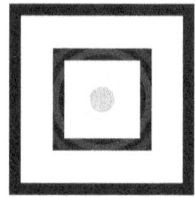

The Coal from the Altar — Part 2

PURIFICATION THROUGH TRIALS

THE COAL DOESN'T JUST warm you; it sears you. Purification is a violent grace. I spent years enduring a series of trials that felt like destruction, but I realize now that God was doing something structural. He wasn't breaking me down; He was clearing the site. He wasn't destroying my future; He was laying the infrastructure for a weight of glory I couldn't yet carry.

The Journey of a First-Generation Pioneer

The path of a first-generation pioneer is unique. It is a journey marked by extreme highs and lows, all anchored by a crushing sense of responsibility to succeed. I had incredible support systems in South Texas. From the Gear Up program in middle school to the VAMOS scholarship funded by Construction Cantu, others had invested heavily in my potential.

I graduated from the University of Texas at Austin with honors, earning a degree in Astronomy with a minor in Latin American Studies. It felt like a fitting tribute to those who had sacrificed for me. But as I stepped into the professional world, the armor began to show its first cracks. I was entering uncharted territory.

The First Loss: The Marketplace

The job market should not have been as difficult as it was, but for a first-generation graduate, every step felt like a potential misstep. I was offered a part-time assistant role at a nonprofit serving university presidents. Simultaneously, I had an interview for a sales position at Dell Latin America. I chose the nonprofit role because the corporate world intimidated me. Looking back, I see that self-doubt was already beginning to cloud my vision.

The assistant role was brutal. I spent my days manually pasting together newsletters from newspaper clippings. I had to tape them down with such precision that no edge marks would appear on the final photocopy. I often wept in frustration. Under the watchful, picky eye of the Executive Director, I struggled to maintain the pace she demanded.

I was spiraling. On paper, I was a Valedictorian and a National Honor Society President. In reality, I was a man who couldn't tape a newsletter straight. I had committed the ultimate error: I tied my identity to my title. Because my title was insignificant, I felt invisible. I was a success story in the making, drowning in the mundane.

The Cycle of Rejection

In a moment of frustration, I quit. I tried a sales job for a business supply company, which involved cold-calling local businesses. Midway through the training, the 'imposter' lie became a physical weight. I didn't just feel it; I tasted it. I ended up in a public bathroom, sick to my stomach, forced to confront the reality that I was chasing a life that wasn't mine. I was trying to validate myself through a system that didn't know my name.

I was humbled. I went back to the nonprofit and begged for my job back. My boss agreed to keep me for only a few weeks. That led to a short stint at United Way. I worked hard, learned the pitch, and supported Fortune 500 corporate accounts. Yet, at the end of the campaign, I was not selected to stay on. The Vice President told me that while they enjoyed my presence, others were stronger representatives.

The algorithms of comparison were loud. Everyone else seemed to be thriving while I was drowning. I was a success story in the making who was currently failing in the real world.

Removing the World's Pattern

This was the lesson of the first loss of self.

God was loosening my grip on my identity; on my worth; on my value. I had been clinging to my accomplishments. I had been clinging to my titles. I had been clinging to my success.

But God was saying, "Arturo, you are not your job title. You are not your accomplishments. You are not your success. You are Mine."

This is the work of the coal. It incinerates the things we use to prop up our ego so we can learn to stand on the Rock alone. God was stripping away the world's pattern, the exhausting cycle of achievement for validation, and replacing it with the Kingdom mandate: **Identity for Assignment**. You don't work to become someone; you work because of who you already are.

The Weight of the Household: Mom's Crisis

The purification intensified when my mother was diagnosed with breast cancer. Because of the complexity of the healthcare system, she had to undergo her initial surgery in Reynosa, Mexico. Navigating that journey as her advocate was a grounding experience. I leveraged every ounce of my network to find resources for her.

Watching her fight taught me to persevere through fear. She is now over a decade in remission. Through her trial, God showed me that the fire does not just purify the individual; it builds the grit necessary to protect a family legacy and navigate failing systems.

■ ■ ■

Biblical Models of Faith Through Trials

The Bible is full of faith refined through trial. These stories are not just ancient history; they are the architectural patterns God still uses to raise up those who will build the systems of a new era.

Job: The Loss of the Hedge

Job was blameless and upright, the greatest man among all the people of the East. Yet, in a single day, he lost his livestock, his servants, his children, and his health. He sat among the ashes and scraped his sores with broken pottery. When his wife urged him to curse God and die, he replied: "Shall we accept good from God, and not trouble?"

This is the pattern of loss: God strips away the "hedge" of protection to reveal the foundation underneath. Job was an "unknown" until his trial revealed a faith that could not be bought or sold. He learned that God is enough even when the provision is gone.

Joseph: The Architect of Supply Chains

Joseph was his father's favorite, but his dreams of greatness led him into a pit. He was sold into slavery, falsely accused of assault, and thrown into an Egyptian prison. He was stripped of freedom, reputation, and position.

But God was with him. Joseph's prison years weren't a delay; they were a laboratory. God was forging the resilience required to manage the logistics of a global famine. Joseph had to learn to steward a prison before he could be trusted to steward an empire. The loss was intentional. It was the only way to build the capacity for a century-level assignment.

Daniel: The Architect of Global Policy

Daniel was a young nobleman carried away to Babylon. He lost his homeland, his family, and even his name. The Babylonians renamed him Belteshazzar to erase his Hebrew identity. He was pressured to conform to a pagan system; yet, Daniel resolved not to defile himself.

His exile was a divine appointment. God was positioning him to be a voice of wisdom in the courts of multiple kings. Daniel survived the lion's den and outlasted multiple empires because his identity was rooted in the Eternal rather than the temporary. The AI era needs "Daniels" who will stand firm in their convictions while stewarding the systems of power with integrity.

David: The Architect of the Cave

David was anointed king as a young man, but he spent years running for his life. He hid in caves and was hunted like an animal. He lost his security and his reputation before he ever held the scepter. But the cave was where David learned to lead a band of outcasts and transform them into a mighty army. He was unknown until his trial refined him for the throne.

The Pattern Is Clear

God purifies through perseverance. He is not being cruel; He is preparing you for the commission. You cannot carry the weight of a global assignment if you are still clinging to the validation of a local title. The systems of this world are designed to shape you in their image, but you must be broken so you can be remade in His.

Joseph, Daniel, and David were not punished by their trials; they were prepared by them. The pit, the prison, the exile, and the cave were the birthplaces of their authority. God is building in you the character to steward the systems of the AI era and the wisdom to navigate geopolitical shifts that would crush a lesser leader.

■ ■ ■

Message to the Unknowns

If you are walking through loss right now, hear me: this is not failure. It is a divine retooling. The fire isn't consuming your future; it is burning away the limitations of your past. God is awakening a hunger in you that will eventually drive you to deliver nations. You aren't falling behind; you are being positioned. You aren't being forgotten; you are being prepared for a seat at the table.

The hardships you face are the very materials God is using to shape you into the leader He has called you to be. You are not just a survivor; you are a pioneer being retooled for a new horizon.

But I Didn't Know

The health crisis of my mother had grounded me. I had been marked by the revival and humbled by the marketplace. I thought I had paid the price. I was wrong. The coal wasn't finished with me. The fire was coming back, and this time, it wouldn't just refine my perspective. It would dismantle my life to rebuild me for the nations.

■ ■ ■

Reflection Questions

1. **What have you lost?** What has God stripped away from you?

2. **What does this loss reveal about your identity?** Are you clinging to titles, accomplishments, or control?

3. **Can you see God's hand in the loss?** Can you trust that He is preparing you, not punishing you?

4. **Who are you without your titles, accomplishments, or control?** Can you say, "I am His"?

5. **Are you willing to be stripped?** Are you willing to be emptied? Are you willing to be broken?

Here Am I, Send Me

THE WEIGHT OF PROPHETIC COMMISSION

"Then I heard the voice of the Lord saying, 'Whom shall I send? And who will go for us?' And I said, 'Here am I. Send me!'"

Isaiah 6:8, NIV

IN OCTOBER 2020, THE vision would not loosen its grip. God had shown me what was coming: the rise of the unknowns, a new billionaire class, and leaders the world had not yet named. I sat at my desk, staring at a blank screen, knowing the message demanded obedience, not polish.

How do you stand in front of people and tell them God showed you names the world has not discovered yet? How do you describe a group of overlooked pioneers who will reshape the global economy and redefine the very nature of wealth?

I had spent twenty years building credibility. Degrees earned. Organizations led. Boards served. But none of it prepared me for this. This was not a strategy I could defend in a boardroom. It was a revelation about a future no spreadsheet could justify. This was a prophetic word about a future that was currently invisible. I felt the crushing weight of it.

The Fear and the Doubt

The questions didn't whisper. They accused me. "Who are you to carry this?"

I had been ordained in 2016 by leaders who recognized the apostolic and prophetic gifting in me. They laid hands on me and commissioned me to advance the Kingdom. Yet, even with that affirmation, I wrestled. I was a strategist and a builder. I knew how to solve problems and design paths. But this vision demanded something else. It required me to speak before proof existed and build before permission was granted.

Then, I remembered Isaiah.

Isaiah saw the Lord high and exalted. He saw his own inadequacy and cried out, "*Woe to me! I am ruined!*" He recognized his disqualification, but God did not leave him in that state. A seraph took a live coal from the altar and touched Isaiah's lips. Purification always precedes the commission.

When God asked, "*Whom shall I send*?" Isaiah didn't negotiate. He didn't ask for clarity or a timeline. Purified lips answered before fear could speak.

My Response: The Unknowns as Builders

I thought about the faces I had seen in the vision. Who were these "unknowns"?

They were border-crossers. People fluent in tension. Builders trained by rejection. First-generation pioneers who had already survived the fire and learned to hear God above every other voice.

By October 2020, I had already stepped away from the systems of men. I moved my family to the Midwest in obedience, not strategy. I wasn't chasing trends. I was positioning myself to father what God was about to release. I was seeking to birth a new model for a world that would emerge by 2030. I did not yet know that ChatGPT would launch two years later, nor did I fully grasp the power of Artificial Intelligence. In hindsight, I recognize that God was raising a new breed of spiritual generals to steward a technological remnant.

I accepted responsibility for them. I said, "*Here am I. Send me.*"

The Mission: Help Them See

My commission was clear. I was sent to confront blindness and teach people to see. The blindness I was addressing was multifaceted:

- **Religious Blindness:** Faith without stewardship. Spirituality without responsibility. They mistake poverty for holiness and never ask who is supposed to fund the Kingdom.

- **Generational Blindness:** Many younger leaders see wealth only as exploitation. They do not perceive that tools like AI and decentralized systems are leveling the playing field. The next billionaire class will be comprised of builders and creators who use technology to serve at scale.

- **Bicultural Blindness:** Border-crossers often see their identity as a liability. They do not see that their ability to translate between cultures and navigate multiple worlds is their greatest "prophetic advantage" in a global economy.

- **Tech-Native Blindness:** Many see AI as a threat of displacement. They do not see it as an instrument of acceleration. These tools will allow the "unknowns" to build in months what used to take years.

■ ■ ■

The Business Case for the Unknowns

This isn't theory. It's already happening. The landscape is shifting in ways that favor the outsider.

1. **The Democratization of Creation:** Generative AI is expected to add trillions to the global economy. This value will be captured by those who deploy these tools to solve real problems, not just those who own the hardware.

2. **The Explosion of the Creator Economy:** We are moving toward a world where individuals can monetize their creativity at scale, bypassing traditional gatekeepers entirely.

3. **The Decentralization of Capital:** Tokenization and crowd-funding are making it possible to raise capital without the permission of traditional banks or venture capitalists.

This is the "***Daniel Strategy***." Daniel was an unknown exile who mastered the wisdom and language of Babylon so thoroughly that he became indispensable to the empire. He did not conform; he outperformed. He mastered the system without bowing to it. Joseph did the same in Egypt, mastering the supply chain of a superpower to save his people.

What You Cannot See Yet

If you are building in obscurity, stop interpreting silence as delay. Here is what you may not yet see:

- **The tools are forming** without your permission.

- **The right people** are being positioned beyond your reach.

- **You cannot see the shift in capital** that is moving away from pedigree and toward merit and impact.

- **Most importantly,** the anointing has outpaced your confidence.

I can see it. God made sure of that.

The Cost of the "Yes"

I said yes, but I did not know the cost. I did not know that saying yes would isolate me before it connected me. I did not know that I would have to carry a message that some would reject with vehemence. I chose to let the call qualify me when my credentials no longer could.

I am asking you the same question: "*Whom shall I send?*"

That burning in your gut is not anxiety; it is anticipation. That restlessness is not a sign of failure; it is a sign of divine design. The "unknowns" are rising. Will you be one of them?

I said yes. A short time later, my world seemed to crumble. Isaiah said yes, and was then told his message would fall on deaf ears and his land would be laid waste. I would soon ask the same question he did: "For how long, Lord?"

I learned that sometimes, God's commission requires you to lose your grip on your current world so that you can reach out and build the next one. The devastation wasn't the end. It was site preparation.

■ ■ ■

Reflection Questions

1. **What is the vision God has shown you** that you have been afraid to speak?

2. **Who are you being called to serve?** Who are the unknowns in your sphere of influence?

3. **What is keeping you from saying, "Here am I. Send me"?** Fear? Doubt? A sense of inadequacy?

4. **What tools, networks, or favor can you not see yet?** What is God positioning you for that you cannot perceive?

5. **Are you willing to say yes**, even if you do not know the cost?

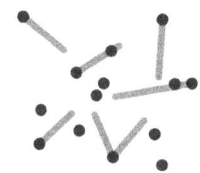

The Valley of Dry Bones

WHEN OBEDIENCE LEADS TO DEVASTATION

"Then I said, 'For how long, Lord?' And he answered: 'Until the cities lie ruined and without inhabitant, until the houses are left deserted and the fields ruined and ravaged.'"

Isaiah 6:11–12, NIV

OBEDIENCE DOES NOT GUARANTEE momentum. Sometimes it drives you straight into the valley. I learned that truth on a Friday morning in June 2025.

I am not revisiting trauma. I am extracting authority from it. The lessons of the valley are the credentials you cannot earn in a boardroom or a university. **For the "unknowns" who will face rejection from investors, partners, and institutions, understand this:** *the valley is not your disqualification.* It is the foundation of everything you are about to build.

■ ■ ■

The End of a Season

I served as CEO of City on a Hill in Milwaukee for more than four years, and I gave it everything I had. My family had sacrificed tremendously to support this mission. We loved the community and poured our lives into the ministry. I believed this role was the culmination of my journey, a place where I could use my strategic skills to serve the overlooked.

After the pandemic, the systems collapsed faster than leadership could adapt. Insurance costs tripled. Facility maintenance became unsustainable. Federal funding stalled for months. The math stopped working, and I hit the limits of what one leader could carry.

My transparency with stakeholders triggered a series of meetings behind closed doors. My wife and I spent those days in deep prayer, navigating sleepless nights and the physical toll of extreme stress. On that final Friday, I met two board officers in a staff lounge. Two cardboard boxes sat in the corner of the room. No one explained them. No one had to.

They terminated me on the spot. The board cited the financial risks involved in my decisions to navigate the chaos. In a suspended heartbeat, I was asked to gather my belongings. I had twenty-five minutes to pack my children's drawings, my books, and my personal items. I was walked out of the building through a back door, where no one could see me.

I placed those boxes in my trunk and drove away in a state of numbing humiliation. This was my exile. This was my ruined city.

Lesson 1: Obedience Guarantees Purpose, Not Comfort

The valley teaches you something obedience never promises: clarity is optional, trust is not. There is a common distortion in our culture that suggests obedience should lead to immediate blessing. Scripture tells a different story. Joseph obeyed and ended up in a prison. Daniel obeyed and ended up in exile. David obeyed and ended up in a cave.

Obedience does not guarantee comfort; it guarantees that you are exactly where God needs you to be. The cost you are paying is not a punishment. It is the positioning required for the commission. For the entrepreneur whose funding falls through or whose co-founder walks away: do not assume you missed God. Assume preparation is underway.

Lesson 2: Identity Beyond the Title

The valley strips away the false self. I was no longer a CEO or a leader of a multimillion-dollar organization. I was Art, sitting in a coffee shop, staring down the question every builder eventually faces: Was I wrong about everything?

The valley forced me to confront a singular question: "Who am I without the platform?" The answer was beautiful in its simplicity: I am a son of God. I am a husband. I am a father. I am a builder. Titles fell away. Identity did not. My identity as an imager remained after the termination.

Lesson 3: The Grace of Community

Isolation is the valley's most dangerous lie. He wants you to believe you are the only one who has failed. But God sends people to keep you above water.

The Sunday following my termination, my wife and I walked into our church, the same place where the October 2020 vision had first manifested. They met us with tears, prayer, and provision. The valley did not take us under. Throughout the following weeks, family and friends provided for us in ways that said, "I see you. I am with you." We were not alone. The valley is not a solo journey; it is a community experience that reveals your true tribe.

Lesson 4: The Clarification of Vision

In the silence of the ruins, the vision from 2020 became sharper. I realized that my time at City on a Hill was not the destination; it was the training ground. God was not resurrecting my old career. He was resurrecting a movement.

As the pressure lifted, revelation rushed back in. I wrote. I listened. I built. The vision demanded a new wineskin, and obedience demanded that I birth it myself.

Lesson 5: Prophesy to the Bones

When everything seems dead, God commands us to prophesy. He asked Ezekiel, "Can these bones live?" Ezekiel gave the only honest answer: "Sovereign Lord, you alone know."

I looked at the ruins of my career and heard the same command: Prophesy. I began to speak out loud the things God had shown me: the rise of the unknowns, the democratization of wealth through AI, and the new breed of inventors who would serve the Kingdom. I launched **Cosmos Renewed** from a valley, not a victory lap. I spoke to the future until breath entered the present.

■ ■ ■

The Birth of Cosmos Renewed

Cosmos Renewed was born in that valley. It exists to help leaders and philanthropists navigate complexity through a Kingdom lens. We focus on three primary domains: community well-being, personalized learning, and regenerative health systems.

This is more than a company; it is an incubator for God-fueled ideas. We use advanced tools, including AI, to help unknown builders design systems that serve people at scale. The launch of this studio was not a "pivot." It was a resurrection. That was the moment the bones stood up.

Your Valley is Your Launchpad

In June 2025, I could not see that my termination was the beginning of a higher commission. I could not see that God was removing a platform I thought I needed so I could build the one He intended.

Your valley qualifies you. If you are sitting among ruins today, do not retreat. Prophesy. Speak until breath answers back.

■ ■ ■

Reflection Questions

1. **What "dry bones" are you sitting among right now?** What seems dead in your life?

2. **Have you experienced a moment when obedience led to devastation instead of success?** How did you respond?

3. **Who are the people God has sent to keep you above water in your valley?** Have you thanked them?

4. **What would it look like for you to "prophesy to the bones"**—to speak life over what seems dead?

5. **Can you honestly say to God, "Sovereign Lord, you alone know"?** What would it take to trust Him with the outcome?

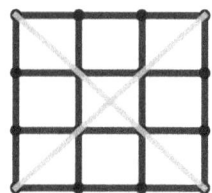

These Bones Can Live

WHEN OBEDIENCE BIRTHS THE NEW

"So I prophesied as he commanded me, and breath entered them;
they came to life and stood up on their feet—a vast army."
Ezekiel 37:10, NIV

EZEKIEL STOOD IN A valley of dry bones and prophesied. He watched as they rattled, came together, and were covered with tendons, flesh, and skin. Then, the breath entered. The bones lived, and the army stood. This was my **Cosmos Renewed** moment.

The Winds of Change

In the valley, God secured my full attention. The summer of 2025 was brutal. It was a season defined by two months of agonizing questions: Had I heard God correctly? Was the October 2020 vision a divine assignment or a personal delusion?

In that silence, something shifted. I had been keeping prayer journals since the move to Milwaukee in July 2020, recording prayers, prophetic words, dreams, visions, and fragments of divine clarity I could not yet understand or situate. Now, in the devastation, the Spirit of God was illuminating those fragments, connecting dots I could not see before, and revealing a pattern I had been too busy to notice.

I flipped through pages from 2019-2023. The themes were consistent: "God reaching the unreachables," "A new move that would awaken America from its slumber and wash her from her sins," and "A new reformation was coming." Not a reformation based on dogma and internal debate, but one that would reform the earth itself.

The lens of the inventor would come forth from God's glory cloud, and out of the Word and Spirit would come creative ideas and inventions. The secrets of creation being revealed in new inventions and patents that would bring transformation in biomedical sciences and beyond, and America being positioned to be a plumbline for the transformation, a vehicle of the freedom to come, and an engine of change.

I stared at those words. I had written them years ago, but I had not fully understood them until now. The new wineskin for me did not emerge at City on a Hill, and it did not come about even in Milwaukee. It had been something set in motion since my grandfather experienced the fire of God and said yes.

The COVID-19 experience had marked my family and me, and the rumblings of the October 2020 encounter had started much earlier. But they began to turn into actionable faith in Oklahoma City, as the Serna family started seeking God together like never before. My move to Milwaukee was a strategic deployment.

The ministry role served as the practical entry point, positioning my family at the epicenter of a new birth. I was initiating a 'bone to bone' alignment required to sustain a global movement. The relocation was the first move in a much larger sequence. Out of our tragic moment of termination, our cries to God began to empower us to prophesy to the four winds. This is how the mission of Cosmos Renewed finally emerged from my inner man.

Your Valley Is Your Incubator

If you are currently sitting in the ruins of a dream, hear this: the valley is not your graveyard; it is your incubator. Devastation is the clarification of your vision. Stripping is not punishment; it is the positioning required for the next level of stewardship. In the valley, God removes what you thought you needed so He can provide what you actually require.

Go back to your journals, your prayers, your prophetic words, and the dreams you had before the noise got loud. What has God been saying all along?

What themes keep appearing? What vision keeps resurfacing, even when you try to ignore it? That is your breath, that is your life, and that is your army waiting to stand.

Prophesy to it.

The PublicLaunch: Starting with Nothing

In August 2025, I publicly launched Cosmos Renewed. I had no salary, no safety net, and no guaranteed clients. I had only obedience and a blind trust that the breath of God would animate a vision I had carried for five years.

I sat at my desk in Milwaukee, staring at a blank business page. My wife served as my emotional lifeline while my children navigated another school year. I was an unemployed leader building a strategic innovation studio for "the unknowns." How do you build a business around a prophetic word? How do you create a blueprint for people you have not yet met?

I did not have a manual, but I knew that obedience precedes results. I wrote the mission, designed the landing page, and reached out to my network. I declared my purpose: "I help leaders navigate complexity, leverage emerging tools, and build sustainable futures." For weeks, the silence was deafening. Then, the first breakthrough arrived.

The First Breakthrough: A Micro-School for the Unknowns

My career has always been about leaders arising with a call to improve the world. This hit home through the concept of the **School of Tyrannus** from **Acts 19**. Paul trained and equipped leaders to carry the message further than he could reach alone.

For two years, Paul taught daily in the lecture hall of Tyrannus, and the result was that "all the Jews and Greeks who lived in the province of Asia heard the word of the Lord" (Acts 19:10, NIV). One man, one school, and an entire region transformed. That was the model, not just preaching to the masses, but raising up world changers who would multiply the impact.

In late 2025, I accepted a founder role for an **Acton Academy** in Greater Milwaukee. This was a Kingdom assignment to raise world-changers and equip the next generation of unknowns. Bone met bone. The school's prototype would leverage the massive shift in technical capability, arming students with the tools to build at the speed of the new era.

The "Holy Smokes" Moment: The AI Accelerant

While I was still in the valley, I encountered the tool that would make the vision of October 2020 achievable. In November 2022, ChatGPT launched. I typed a simple prompt regarding a strategic plan for a nonprofit. In seconds, a coherent, detailed outline appeared. I stared at the screen and recognized I was holding fire.

This tool arrived as the accelerant for the October 2020 vision. The timing was precise. God revealed the mandate in 2020 and released the capability in 2022. The barriers to entry collapsed.

I spent the next few days experimenting, writing prompts, refining outputs, and testing the limits. I asked it to draft donor communications, to create program evaluation frameworks, to generate budget scenarios, and to write job descriptions. Every time, it delivered.

I spent three years mastering these tools: ChatGPT, Claude, Gemini, and Midjourney. I eventually participated in the **gener8tor Generative AI for Leaders** program, which confirmed my suspicion: the barriers to entry are collapsing. The tools of the elite were now in the hands of the unknowns.

The Practical Manual: A Toolkit for the Unknowns

This is not theory. This is the "how-to" for the new class of Kingdom builders.

Category	Emerging Tools	The Shift
Software Development	GitHub Copilot, Cursor, Replit	You no longer need a team of developers; you can code with natural language.
Brand & Design	Midjourney, DALL-E, Ideogram	A single founder can create a $50,000 brand identity for $20 a month.
Marketing & Strategy	Claude, Jasper, Perplexity	Professional copy and market research that once took months now takes hours.
Operations	Airtable, Notion, Zapier	No-code platforms allow small teams to manage enterprise-level systems.
Product Launch	Bubble, FlutterFlow, Framer	Non-technical founders can build and launch apps without an engineering degree.

Table 7.1: The Unknown's Toolkit — Leveraging Emerging Technology to Democratize High-Level Systems.

The gatekeepers have lost their authority. Vision, technical literacy, and radical obedience now outweigh traditional credentials. The tools are in your hands. Your willingness to build is the only remaining variable.

■ ■ ■

The Shift Is Happening: Case Studies of the Unknowns

The Forbes list is being rewritten. Let us look at the proof.

Case Study 1: The Blueprint of an Unknown - The Jan Koum Story

Jan Koum weaponized his history. His childhood in a Soviet surveillance state served as the research and development phase for WhatsApp. He transformed the silence of his youth into a global standard for privacy. He hijacked his education from a local library. Rejection from Facebook provided the liberation he needed to build a $19 billion empire.

The Crucible

Born in 1976 in Soviet-era Kyiv, Jan Koum's childhood was defined by scarcity and silence. His home was a small apartment without hot water. Life was a landscape where the government monitored every phone call and privacy was an unaffordable luxury. He was being prepared in a hidden place of restriction for a future of global connection.

In 1992, sixteen-year-old Koum and his mother fled to Mountain View, California. They left his father behind, a separation that eventually became permanent. America offered freedom, but it did not immediately offer comfort. While his mother battled a cancer diagnosis, they survived on the fringes of society. They relied on welfare, food stamps, and government housing. To keep the lights on, Koum swept floors as a grocery store janitor. He watched through the storefront glass as his peers drove cars he could not afford. He was not just living in poverty; he was being forged by it.

The Self-Taught Architect

Koum hijacked his education from a local library. Armed with used manuals from local libraries, he taught himself computer programming. He joined an elite hacking collective known as **w00w00**, where he found a community of outsiders who prioritized skill over credentials. Though he enrolled at San Jose State University, the traditional classroom could not keep pace with his drive. He dropped out to join Yahoo as an infrastructure engineer.

It was there he met Brian Acton. Bonded by a mutual disdain for corporate bureaucracy and the status quo, the duo eventually walked away from Yahoo in 2007. They spent a year backpacking across South America to clear their heads and seek a new vision. Upon their return, they both applied for jobs at Facebook. Both were rejected. That rejection was the catalyst. It did not just sting; it liberated them to build their own world.

The Spark of Necessity

In 2009, the iPhone sparked a technological revolution, but Koum saw something deeper than a gadget. He saw a solution to the trauma of his youth. Communication was still a predatory industry. International calls to Ukraine were extortionate, SMS was limited, and privacy was non-existent. He recognized a "Kingdom-sized" problem that needed a simplified solution.

On February 24, 2009, his thirty-third birthday, Koum shared his vision with Acton over a game of ultimate frisbee. He envisioned a messaging app that was free, simple, and impenetrable. That day, **WhatsApp Inc.** was born. It was an act of "prophesying to the bones" of his own difficult past.

From Failure to Explosion

The launch was initially a disaster. The early version was clunky and largely ignored by the masses. Koum nearly quit, but the release of iOS 3.0 changed the trajectory of the company. By leveraging the new push notification feature, Koum pivoted. He realized people did not just want another app; they wanted a digital lifeline that felt like a real-time conversation.

By 2011, WhatsApp was a top-tier contender. By 2014, it was a global phenomenon with 450 million active users. It succeeded because it was built on Koum's non-negotiable, Soviet-era convictions: No ads. No games. No gimmicks. Just pure privacy. He had taken his "bicultural wound" and turned it into a global standard for security.

The $19 Billion Circle

In February 2014, Mark Zuckerberg came calling. Facebook, the very company that had rejected Koum five years earlier, acquired WhatsApp for $19 billion.

Koum made one final, poetic demand. The signing would not happen at a corporate headquarters or a high-rise law firm. Instead, he drove to the North County Social Services office. This was the same building where he had once stood in line to receive food stamps. On the door of that welfare office, he signed the papers that made him one of the wealthiest men on earth. It was not a stunt; it was a testament. The unknown had risen, and the "last" had truly become "first."

The Blueprint: Lessons for the Ambitious

- **Your History is Your Credential**: Koum's background in a surveillance state was the foundation of the encryption that changed the world. The pain you have lived is the problem you are uniquely qualified to solve.

- **Solve Lived Problems:** Innovation is not about chasing a trend; it is about ending a personal frustration. The most valuable systems are born from necessity rather than vanity.

- **Principles Over Profit**: Koum famously refused to sell user data, even under immense pressure from investors. Integrity is not just a moral choice; it is a competitive advantage.

- **Rejection is Redirection**: A closed door is often a pivot toward a larger destiny. If Facebook had hired Koum in 2009, the global system of WhatsApp would never have existed.

- **Leverage the Current**: Koum did not wait for perfect conditions. He saw the tools available, the iPhone and the App Store, and he built. The tools of the AI era are in your hands right now. The only question is: Will you use them?

■ ■ ■

Case Study 2: Brendan Foody, Adarsh Hiremath, and Surya Midha - The 22-Year-Old Billionaires

In March 2025, three friends became the youngest self-made billionaires in history. Their journey serves as definitive proof that the unknowns are rising with a velocity previously unimagined. They applied the discipline of high school debate to dismantle the traditional recruiting industry. They scaled a global network using a lean team and superior logic. Their success proves that execution renders age irrelevant. They rode the crest of the wave.

Brendan Foody, Adarsh Hiremath, and Surya Midha, the co-founders of the AI-powered recruiting platform Mercor, raised $350 million at a $10 billion valuation. Overnight, with each founder holding roughly 22 percent of the company, their individual net worth exceeded $2 billion. In doing so, they dethroned Mark Zuckerberg, who achieved billionaire status at twenty-three.

The Beginning

Foody, Hiremath, and Midha met at Bellarmine College Preparatory, a Jesuit high school in San Jose. They were not the campus elites; they were the "debate nerds." They spent late nights preparing for national tournaments, a process that forced them to think with precision, argue persuasively, and analyze complex problems under extreme pressure. These specific skills, honed in obscurity, would eventually become the foundation of their global success.

After graduation, they scattered to elite universities. Foody and Midha went to Georgetown to study economics and foreign service, while Hiremath went to Harvard for computer science. Despite the geographical distance, they remained connected. They texted constantly, shared emerging ideas, and dreamed of building a system together. In early 2023, during their sophomore years, they launched Mercor. The initial concept was a simple online marketplace connecting skilled software engineers in India with U.S. startups in need of affordable remote talent. They saw themselves as the bridge between two worlds.

The Pivot

Within months, however, they recognized a much larger opportunity emerging in the glory cloud of the AI boom. Companies like OpenAI, Anthropic, and Google DeepMind were racing to build foundational models. These models faced a critical bottleneck: they required human-in-the-loop feedback to improve. The algorithms needed humans to label data, simulate scenarios, and provide the nuanced judgment that software cannot replicate. Demand for this specialized feedback was skyrocketing.

Mercor pivoted. Rather than merely connecting coders, they built an AI-powered platform designed to automate high-level recruitment. They delivered a global network of over 30,000 vetted specialists, including lawyers, doctors, and researchers, who were paid to refine the world's most advanced AI models. Their client list soon included the titans of the industry: OpenAI, Anthropic, Google DeepMind, and six of the "Magnificent Seven" tech giants.

The Growth

By mid-2024, Mercor's annualized revenue hit $500 million, a staggering leap from the $100 million recorded just months prior. All three founders received the Thiel Fellowship, which provided a $100,000 grant to drop out of college and focus exclusively on their mission. They accelerated their funding rounds at a pace that left the traditional market breathless:

- **September 2024:** Raised $32 million in a Series A round at a $250 million valuation.

- **February 2025:** Raised $100 million in a Series B round at a $2 billion valuation.

- **March 2025:** Raised $350 million in a Series C round at a $10 billion valuation.

The company was operated by a lean team of only thirty people. The median age of the entire staff was twenty-two.

Key Lessons from Foody, Hiremath, and Midha

- **Skills translate from unexpected places.** Debate tournaments were their "School of Tyrannus." The discipline of thinking under pressure built a $10 billion company. Your background, no matter how niche, is your unique prophetic advantage.

- **Pivot when you perceive market demand.** The founders were not married to their original marketplace idea. They followed the "breath" of the market into AI. Flexibility is a vital competitive advantage for the unknown.

- **Lean teams scale through technology.** Thirty people generated $500 million in revenue because they used AI to automate the mundane. You do not need a massive headcount to have a massive impact.

- **Age is irrelevant when execution is undeniable.** The unknowns are rising regardless of their birth year. The critical question is not your age but the speed at which you can move and adapt.

- **Move while the wave is forming.** Foody, Hiremath, and Midha saw the AI wave and acted immediately. The tools are present, the market is ready, and the opportunity is waiting for those willing to step out.

■ ■ ■

The Unknowns Are Rising: The Pattern Is Clear

Jan Koum, Brendan Foody, Adarsh Hiremath, and Surya Midha are part of a growing pattern. The vision from October 2020 was never a matter of wishful thinking. It was a prophetic insight into an unfolding economic reality. Today, the unknowns are rising because the tools are present and the traditional barriers have dissolved. This is not mere theory or hype. It is a documented shift in the global landscape.

The Forbes list is being rewritten in real time. Wealth is shifting, and the old gatekeepers are losing their grip on the entry points of industry. This transformation is occurring faster than any analyst predicted.

The Role of Mentors and Faith-Driven Communities

The unknowns cannot rise in a vacuum. They require mentors to ground them in foundational principles of divine wisdom, the timeless ethical blueprints that govern a life of integrity. These mentors teach divine strategy as a practical business methodology. They hold builders accountable to a standard of purity and blamelessness that protects them from the traps of the traditional Silicon Valley mindset.

Faith-driven communities serve as the essential ecosystems where these callings are nurtured. These environments do not just celebrate financial exits; they disciple the hearts of the builders. They do not merely fund ideas; they steward divine assignments. The unknowns need communities that reinforce a revolutionary truth: wealth is a tool, not a destination. In this economy, success is measured by Kingdom impact, and the ultimate reward is the approval of the Creator.

The Core Strategy: Seek First His Kingdom

The unknowns do not build for their own glory. Their core strategy is rooted in the foundational promise of **Matthew 6:33, NIV**: "But seek first his kingdom and his righteousness, and all these things will be given to you as well." This is not a religious footnote. It is the non-negotiable bedrock of their enterprise.

The distinction between the rising unknowns and secular founders, who often view technology as the ultimate savior and wealth as the primary goal, is one of origin and intent. We are extending a Kingdom. The unknowns rise on the strength of a divine summons. We anchor our success in a non-negotiable guardrail: **Seek First.** Success that costs you your soul is a total loss. We build to reform the system, not to be colonized by it.

When a builder prioritizes the Kingdom, they design systems that restore human dignity and deploy technology to serve the collective good. They refuse to compromise their values for the sake of venture capital. They do not sacrifice their families for the sake of growth. By seeking the Kingdom first, they ensure that their success does not cost them their souls. These guardrails are not restrictive rules, but rather life-giving rhythms of a healthy spirit.

The Guardrails: What Keeps the Unknowns Faithful?

We are witnessing a generational movement. Gen Z and those following are responding to the visible failure of modern institutions and secular humanism to heal the world's pain. They have seen the empty promises of technology without ethics and wealth without a "why." They are hungry for a foundation that is both real and eternal.

God is raising them up to build systems that do not merely generate profit, but actively expand the order and peace of His Kingdom on earth.

■ ■ ■

Beauty from Ashes

By late 2025, the digital presence of **Cosmos Renewed** began to move the metrics of impact. We grew from a standstill to sixty registered followers. Our content reached over five hundred impressions with more than one hundred and fifty unique visitors. I finally had visibility, an entry point, and tangible momentum.

The **Acton Academy in Greater Milwaukee** concepts were taking shape. The **gener8tor program** was arming me with the technical proficiency to lead in the AI era. The press release was circulating, and a strategic network was forming. The "dry bones" were clearly coming to life.

However, I was still building in relative isolation. I was carrying the vision and prophesying to the bones, but I had not yet connected with the full army of Kingdom inventors I was called to shape. That was the next phase of the divine plan. God was about to show me exactly how He gathers the remnant for the work ahead.

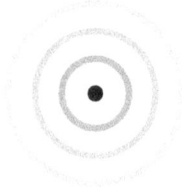

The Holy Seed

THE REMNANT EMERGES

"And though a tenth remains in the land, it will again be laid waste. But as the terebinth and oak leave stumps when they are cut down, so the holy seed will be the stump in the land."

Isaiah 6:13, NIV

EVEN AFTER DEVASTATION, A remnant remains. Whether it is a tenth, a stump, or a holy seed, this is the promise: the vision does not die. It merely goes underground to gather the nutrients required to sprout into a new era.

The Monday Night Encounter

In the fall of 2025, I returned to Pewaukee, Wisconsin, the very city where I received the October 2020 vision. I was invited to speak at a gathering of worshipers, a moment that felt like a full-circle assignment. Our team encouraged this "victorious remnant" to hold fast to the prophetic blueprint of the future.

At the conclusion, a young man approached me. He was tall, brown-skinned, with a purposely likable and inquisitive presence. He had traveled from Illinois with his mother, drawn by my background as an executive leader at Teach For America and a ministry CEO. He was a junior in high school, and he had a question: Would I guide him as he mapped out his post-graduation future?

I prayed over him. I affirmed God's call and destiny for his generation, while praying for courage and clarity for the path ahead.

The Passion of the Unknown

As I spoke with him and his mother, his passion became clear. He is a builder of online games. More importantly, he wants to use those games to help his peers navigate the trauma of this culture—stress, depression, and rejection. He wants to take the lessons of his own journey and use his technical talents to further the light of Christ.

I sensed God's confirmation immediately: *Help him become*. My success was never the goal. My assignment is to identify the holy seeds and teach them to perceive the shift God is orchestrating through technology and spirit. I am a scout for the unknowns.

We have since begun a journey of virtual mentorship, carving out his purpose statement as a future founder. He is an "unknown" rising. This encounter reaffirmed the mission of the October 2020 vision. It was never about my success; it was about identifying the "holy seeds" in the land and helping them perceive what God is doing through technology and spirit.

Your Role: Helping the Remnant See

Isaiah's commission was difficult. He was told to speak to a people who would be "ever hearing, but never understanding". However, a remnant always remains. Your job as a Kingdom entrepreneur is not just to build a business or create wealth; it is to find the "stumps" and plant seeds.

The **collaborative ecosystem** is governed by a single law: A rising tide lifts all boats. Hoarding knowledge is a strategy for the old world. In the new era, you invest in the community to secure your own success. You build the network before you build the product. You rise by lifting others, or you don't rise at all.

The new billionaire class will understand and appreciate this. They will build networks before they build products. They will share knowledge before they hoard it. They will rise by lifting others. However, this collaborative spirit requires a foundation of intentional guidance; to lead this new era effectively, you must act as the catalyst that awakens their higher purpose.

You must help them:

- **See** the potential God has placed within them.

- **Hear** the specific calling on their life.

- **Perceive** the massive technological and spiritual shift happening right now.

While the scale of this shift is global, the engine of its transformation is not found in the masses, but in the concentrated power of a dedicated few, a principle woven throughout the fabric of scripture.

■ ■ ■

Biblical Models of the Remnant

God rarely needs a majority to transform a system. He requires only a faithful few:

- **Noah's Eight:** From only eight people, the earth was repopulated after the flood.

- **Gideon's 300:** God reduced an army of 32,000 down to 300 to ensure the victory was attributed to His power rather than human strength.

- **Elijah's 7,000:** When the prophet felt alone, God revealed He had reserved 7,000 who had not compromised their integrity.

- **Jesus' 12:** Christ invested three years in twelve ordinary men, a remnant that eventually birthed the largest movement in human history.

In the modern age, this ancient strategy of the "faithful few" has found its digital mirror in the way information now flows across the globe.

The Open-Source Revolution

Knowledge has escaped the gatekeepers. In the new era, sharing is the primary currency of influence. Linus Torvalds proved this with Linux. By releasing his code, he didn't lose power; he decentralized it. Today, that code runs the world. Hoarding is a liability; collaboration is an accelerant.

The same pattern repeats across industries. Arduino democratized electronics. Wikipedia democratized knowledge. GitHub democratized code collaboration. Each platform proves that sharing accelerates innovation faster than hoarding.

Cross-Border Collaboration

Geography no longer limits your reach. A developer in rural Mexico now has access to the same coding libraries as an engineer at Google. Diversity is no longer a buzzword, it is a competitive advantage. When a coder in Poland partners with a designer in Brazil, they see problems that a homogeneous team would miss.

I have experienced the transformative power of this ecosystem firsthand. Before the global lockdowns of COVID, my work with Teach For All drew me to Kathmandu for a global leadership conference. In the rural classrooms and winding paths of small Nepali communities, I sat with local fellows and listened to the raw, personal stories of those serving on the front lines of education.

Those relationships fundamentally shifted my understanding of leadership and impact. By immersing myself in contexts vastly different from my own, I witnessed ingenious solutions I never could have imagined, solutions born of necessity and brilliance. The relational lessons gained in Nepal continue to serve as the bedrock of my work today.

My journey into collaborative networks didn't end there; it expanded through communities like Adria Dunn's **The Vine Global**, Wes Chapman's **The Human Gathering**, and Tarja Stephens' **Leaders of the Future**. These environments demolished traditional silos, connecting me with a tapestry of leaders across every imaginable industry, age group, and continent.

The common thread? A commitment to rise by lifting others.

Strategic Mentorship: Compressing Time

Mentorship is a time-compression tool. It collapses years of trial and error into hours of strategic insight.

1. **Moses and Jethro (The Consultant):** Jethro, a Midianite priest, gave Moses the blueprint for a distributed governance model, saving him from burnout. This proves that cross-border connections provide the "outside" perspective needed to scale.

2. **Paul and Timothy (The Successor):** Paul recognized Timothy's bi-cultural identity as a bridge-building asset. Their relationship was not

tactical; it was a deeply relational investment in the next generation.

3. **Esther and Mordecai (The Strategist):** Mordecai coached Esther to leverage her "royal position" to save her people. He helped her see her purpose when she was paralyzed by fear.

I have stood on the shoulders of giants throughout my journey. For the unknowns to rise, they must leverage the wisdom of those who have already cleared the path. To remain credible and accountable in the marketplace, we must acknowledge the voices that shaped our character before they shaped our careers.

The Pillars of My Path: The Power of Mentorship

I have benefited from extraordinary mentors who modeled the intersection of spiritual integrity and strategic excellence. **Bob and Leslie Long**, based in San Marcos, Texas, were a primary architects of my leadership philosophy. They curated a network of relational leaders who operated within a distinct biblical paradigm. Bob taught me that true leadership has little to do with titles or tactics; instead, it is built upon the bedrock of character and the selfless service of others.

Together they modeled the principle of rising by lifting others. They connected people with intentionality, shared their wisdom with a loose hand, and invested in younger leaders without any expectation of a return. Their influence remains a primary compass for how I lead today.

In the same way, **Ronnie and Gail Long**, the leaders of Freedom's Fire Ministry in Texas, provided the life counsel that shaped my understanding of team dynamics. They taught me how to forge high-capacity teams committed to advancing the Kingdom of God among the nations. Some of the leadership traits I value most today, visionary grit and spiritual alignment, were first nurtured under their seasoned guidance.

Global Innovation and Values-Based Leadership

Beyond these foundational spiritual mentors, I have learned from a global network of innovators. These are the individuals who opened doors to angel investors, the coders who sharpened my technical proficiency, and the entrepreneurs who shared the hard-won lessons of scaling a business in a volatile market.

While their industries and backgrounds varied, the common thread was undeniable. Each of these mentors led with values first. They checked their egos at the door and arrived with humble, servant hearts. Their primary focus was never the mere accumulation of wealth; they were focused on improving the condition of humanity rather than simply building their own empires.

This is the specific brand of mentorship that fuels the inventor revolution. It is not found in transactional networking or social climbing for personal gain. It is found in authentic connections where people genuinely and sacrificially invest in the success of another.

■ ■ ■

The Bridge Role: The Barnabas Anointing

Leaders over fifty are the strategic bridges of this movement. You are the 'Barnabas' generation. Your role is to vouch for the unknowns and deploy your network capital to open doors they cannot yet reach. Your wisdom is the credential the next generation requires.

Barnabas was the bridge that introduced the "unknown" Paul to the fearful leaders in Jerusalem.

Your role is to:

- **Vouch** for the unknowns when others doubt them.

- **Deploy** your decades of network capital to open doors they cannot reach.

- **Stand in the gap** between established resources and emerging vision.

Your wisdom is the credential this generation cannot manufacture. You are the Barnabas they are waiting for.

Practical Exercise: Mapping Your Ecosystem

You cannot improve what you do not measure. To build a Kingdom-era system, you must audit your network.

1. **Map Current Connections:** List 20 people you can call for advice today.

2. **Domain Audit:** Do your connections span technology, finance, education, and healthcare?

3. **Diversity Check:** Do you have intergenerational and cross-cultural relationships?

4. **Identify Gaps:** Where do you lack access? Do you need an AI expert? An angel investor?

5. **Action Plan:** Make three new strategic connections this month to fill those gaps.

This exercise reveals your network's current state. Now you can act strategically to fill gaps.

Filling the Gaps

Once you identify gaps, create a plan to fill them. If you lack technical expertise, join coding communities. Attend hackathons. Contribute to open-source projects. Engage with developers online.

If you need investor connections, attend startup events. Join angel investor networks. Engage with investors on X and LinkedIn. Share your progress publicly to attract attention.

If you lack cross-cultural connections, join global networks. Attend international conferences (virtual or in-person). Partner with organizations working across borders.

Be intentional. Set goals. Aim to make three new strategic connections per month. Follow up consistently. Nurture relationships over time.

Remember, networking is not about collecting contacts. It is about building genuine relationships. Quality beats quantity every time.

The Seed is Rising

The remnant is emerging. Whether it is a gamer in Illinois or a coder in Lagos, the "unknowns" are standing up. They are the holy seed remaining in the land. Our mission is to see them, hear them, and help them perceive their divine design.

The world will never be the same.

■ ■ ■

Reflection Questions

1. **Identify the Holy Seed:** Who in your sphere carries a divine blueprint for innovation? If you are a mentor, name the specific barrier you will dismantle for them this week. If you are an Unknown, identify the community where you are currently visible to those who can affirm your rise.

2. **Execute the Barnabas Assignment:** To whom are you called to be a bridge? Identify one "Paul" in your network, high potential, low access, and vouch for their character to a key stakeholder before this month ends. Your reputation is the currency of their entry.

3. **Map the Structural Gaps:** Identify the most significant vacancy in your network. Do you lack a technical co-laborer, a strategic elder, or a peer-level collaborator? Name the specific community you will join this week to fill that void.

4. **Confront the Pedigree Trap:** Are you limiting your impact to those who fit a specific background? Risk your reputation on someone who lacks the traditional pedigree but carries the divine anointing to build.

5. **Operationalize "Seek First":** Does your moral framework dictate your decisions, or is it a footnote? Identify one area where you will prioritize Kingdom impact over short-term market capitalization. Integrity is your competitive advantage.

6. **Locate the Emerging Evidence:** Where is the "stump" sprouting in your industry? List three tangible signs that the remnant is emerging and align your resources with that momentum today.

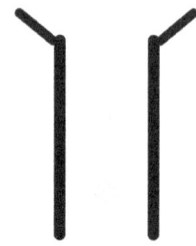

The Deployment

FROM OBSCURITY TO AUTHORITY

"Do you have eyes but fail to see, and ears but fail to hear?"
Mark 8:18, NIV

JESUS DIRECTED HIS MOST piercing question to His inner circle, not the elite. He challenged the very men who walked with Him to wake up to the reality standing in their midst. This is the mandate for every leader reading these words: You must see what God is orchestrating. You must hear the call above the market noise. You must perceive the shift.

The 2020 Vision: A Kingdom Movement

The vision I received in October 2020 was never merely about economics or the accumulation of wealth. It was a prophetic window into the Kingdom of Heaven breaking into the earth. Jesus utilized parables to describe this exponential, pervasive influence:

- **The Mustard Seed:** The Kingdom begins as the smallest of seeds but grows into a tree large enough to support the birds of the air.

- **The Yeast:** The Kingdom works like leaven, silently and persistently transforming the entire batch of dough.

The remnant rising today is a *"Founder Army"* of chosen vessels. They will not be governed by the traditional ideologies of socialism, communism, or capitalism. They will be altogether different. They will build, create, and heal from the supernatural realm, anchored in the values of their Maker. The zeal of the Lord will consume them; that which they set their mind, heart, and hand to will fill the earth and multiply with great acceleration.

The Hardwiring of Self-Serving Structures

Systemic blindness obscures this movement from the masses. Self-serving structures—education, entertainment, and religious institutions—have hardwired us to seek personal comfort while ignoring the **Gospel of the Kingdom**. We have been discipled by hierarchies that fear the rise of a godly remnant. Joseph and Daniel prove that you can architect new systems in the heart of a pagan world. The kingdom creates a realm, the kingdom creates a people, but the kingdom of God is not synonymous with its realm or its people.

The Blueprints of Joseph and Daniel

Joseph and Daniel built the infrastructure of kingdoms, not merely survived within them.

- **Joseph:** He rose from a prisoner to a prime minister in a single day. He did not just interpret a dream; he designed a system that saved nations from famine. He managed resources and positioned his family for the fulfillment of a divine promise.

- **Daniel:** He maintained his identity in the heart of Babylon. He served pagan kings with such excellence that he was found to be ten times better than the experts of his day. He influenced policy and saw visions of the eternal Kingdom.

The "Unknowns" rising today are the Josephs and Daniels of the AI era. They will not just build companies; they will steward systems for the glory of God.

The Three Barriers to Seeing

To rise, the Unknowns must break through three specific forms of blindness.

1. **Cultural Blindness: Reject the lie of 'people like us.'** This is internalized oppression disguised as safety. God qualifies the chosen. Your bicultural identity is your primary competitive advantage.

2. **Theological Blindness: Reject the lie of worldly wealth.** Reject the poverty gospel that equates lack with holiness. Wealth is a tool. The new billionaire class is formed in the fear of the Lord, prioritizing the Kingdom over the market cap.

3. **Practical Blindness: Reject the lie of scarcity.** The democratization of tools has rendered the 'lack of network' excuse obsolete. Jan Koum and the Mercor founders proved that vision outweighs a pedigree.

The Healing: How to Open Your Eyes

Healing requires your participation. You must choose to see, hear, and perceive.

- **SEE the Evidence:** Analyze the Forbes list. Legacy wealth is retreating as self-made unknowns seize the territory.

- **HEAR the Assignment:** Silence the critics and listen to the pain of the community. That pain is your market entry point.

- **PERCEIVE the Advantage:** Recognize wealth creation as a learnable skill. Your border-crossing background provides the intuition that AI cannot replicate.

Start Now. Start Small. Start Scared.

You do not need a perfect plan; you need a willing spirit. Fear is not a sign of failure, but rather a sign that you are stepping into something bigger than yourself. There is a problem that only you can solve and a legacy that only you can leave.

This vision is for the generations after you. I look at my children and I see builders and innovators. I am building for people I will never meet. Like Abraham, we may not see the full fulfillment of the promise in our lifetime, but we are planting the "Holy Seed" that will become a nation.

■ ■ ■

An Invitation to the Holders of Wealth

Holders of current wealth: You are being summoned to steward resources for a new era. This is your Barnabas moment. Deploy your capital into the prototypes of the future.

1. **Invest in the School:** Acton Academy Greater Milwaukee is a prototype for raising world-changers.

2. **Invest in the Studio:** Cosmos Renewed is the incubator finding and equipping the rising remnant.

3. **Invest in the Vision:** Buy this book for your peers and your grandchildren. Build the infrastructure for the generation you will never meet.

God is moving. The unknowns are rising, and the wave that moves them is the wind of the Spirit. For there is a cause, and God has released His plans for the new era. Let's walk through the door of hope and join Him.

As Daniel saw the kingdoms of this world becoming the Kingdom of our Lord and of His Messiah, we are called into that holy vision once again. Trusting that the glory of God will be seen in an unprecedented manner outside of the usual four walls of the church building.

A Blessing for the Commissioned

Father, I stand as a father in the faith. I speak a blessing over the commissioned Unknowns and their champions.

To the Unknowns: I bless you with clarity of vision. May you see what God is calling you to build. I bless you with the spirit of Joseph to steward wealth with integrity and the spirit of Daniel to influence empires with excellence. I bless you with the spirit of Esther to leverage your position "for such a time as this" and the spirit of David to defeat the giants others fear. I bless you with favor; may doors open that no man can shut. I bless you with the zeal of the Lord—may it consume you and sustain you.

To the Mentors and Bridge Builders: I bless you with the spirit of Barnabas to vouch for the Unknowns when others doubt. I bless you with the spirit of Jethro to offer scalable wisdom and the spirit of Mordecai to provide strategic positioning. I bless you with the spirit of Paul to mentor deeply and relationally. I bless you with a long view that invests in generational legacy.

To all who are reading: I bless you with the courage to say, "Here am I. Send me." I bless you with the faith to start now, start small, and start scared. May you trust that the glory of God will be seen in unprecedented ways outside the four walls of the church.

In the name of Jesus, the King of Kings, I release this blessing over you. Amen.

Your Invitation to Shine

You are not an accident. You are not a mistake. You are exactly who God needs you to be to build what He is calling you to build. The window of opportunity is open, and the tools are available. The only question remains: Will you step through the door?

The world is waiting. Your family is waiting. God is waiting. It is your invitation to shine.

Here am I. Send me.

Will you say it? Will you mean it? Will you live it?

The unknowns are rising. Your name could be next.

■ ■ ■

Reflection Questions

1. **Confront the Barrier:** Of the three primary forms of blindness—cultural, theological, or practical—which is currently exerting the most influence over your decision-making? Identify one specific "lie" you have internalized that prevents you from seeing yourself as a Kingdom-era builder.

2. **Audit the Evidence:** Beyond the case studies of Jan Koum or Mercor, what evidence have you observed in your own industry or community that the "unknowns" are rising? List three names of individuals or organizations that represent this shift.

3. **Identify the Lived Problem:** What specific pain or injustice have you experienced that you are uniquely positioned to solve through technology or innovation? How does this problem align with the needs of the "overlooked" in your generation?

4. **Evaluate Your Council:** Who are the specific mentors or "bridge builders" God has sent to speak life over your calling? Have you allowed their perspective to override the fear-based "wisdom" of your existing culture?

5. **Draft Your Commission:** Using the "Here am I" framework, write your personal commission statement. Be specific: To whom are you sent, what are you building, and what is the intended Kingdom impact?

6. **Take the First Step:** Faith without participation remains a vision only. What is one concrete, "start small" action you will take within the next 48 hours to move toward your divine assignment?

Appendix A: The Keys to the Kingdom

A PRACTICAL GUIDE TO RECLAIMING YOUR CREATIVE POWER AND BUILDING WEALTH IN THE NEW ERA

The Permission Trap

I REMEMBER THE FIRST time someone told me I needed permission to build something that mattered.

I was 19. Fresh out of high school and working as an AmeriCorps member in South Texas. I had an idea for streamlining how we connected youth to creative resources. Cut processing time in half while serving twice as many people with the same budget.

My supervisor listened politely. Then said: "That's interesting. But we'd need approval from the director. And buy-in from program staff at the youth center. Probably not likely."

The idea died in discussion.

I watched this pattern repeat for two decades. Brilliant ideas suffocated by gatekeepers. Talented people told to wait their turn. Communities solving their own problems, then being told their solutions didn't fit the approved framework.

For most of human history, wealth creation required permission. You needed access to capital. Geographic proximity to opportunity. Institutional credentials. Family connections. The right last name.

Banks decided who received loans. Universities decided who received degrees. Publishers decided whose ideas got shared. Venture capitalists decided which businesses got funded. Corporations decided who climbed the ladder.

The system worked beautifully for those already inside. For everyone else, the gates stayed closed.

The Shift: From Gatekeepers to Networks

Then something changed in my perspective.

I read *New Power* by Jeremy Heimans and Henry Timms during my time with Teach For America in Oklahoma City. The book mapped how technology and social media were democratizing voice, giving individuals the power to build movements without institutional permission.

Sometimes for good. The Arab Spring. Grassroots fundraising for disaster relief. Communities organizing around shared problems. Sometimes not for good. Misinformation campaigns. Mob justice. Echo chambers amplifying division.

But the genie was out of the bottle. The power to organize, create, and build was no longer locked behind institutional gates.

> **Then came generative AI.** ChatGPT launched in November 2022. Within two months, 100 million users. The fastest-growing consumer application in history.

Suddenly, expertise was democratized. A high school student in rural Texas could access the same AI tools as a Stanford MBA. A single mom in Milwaukee could build a business plan without hiring consultants. An immigrant entrepreneur could prototype products without an engineering degree.

This was the window I had seen in the vision. The moment when technology caught up with the aspirations of people who had been locked out. The deep hunger I felt transitioning from Mexico to the United States. The learning curve. The grit. The resilience. The fire lit in me, my brothers, our family.

It came full circle. Leveraging technology to create a new class of wealth builders. Not for venture capital returns. Not for shareholders. Not even primarily for themselves. But because it's fundamental to their existence. Their well-being. Their people. They get to define who this is.

Case Study: Nepal's Youth Revolution (September 2025)

Consider what happened in Nepal. Youth-led protests erupted across the nation. Gen Z activists, fed up with government corruption and social media crackdowns, organized massive demonstrations. Within 48 hours, the government collapsed. Iconic buildings burned. The prime minister resigned.

One young activist declared: *"This is not just about social media. It is about demanding a fair and just Nepal where our voices actually count."*

Another leader spoke at the UN General Assembly, demanding *"nothing less than a transparent and corruption-free future."*

This movement succeeded because of networks. Young Nepalis connected across cities through **WhatsApp** and **social media**. They coordinated protests. They shared strategies. They amplified each other's voices. Technology enabled collaboration that toppled entrenched power structures.

The lesson for inventors is clear: *Networks matter more than credentials.* When you connect people across borders, you create movements. When you build trust across cultures, you unlock collective power that no individual possesses alone.

■ ■ ■

The Perfect Storm: Why This Moment Matters

Several forces converged to create this window:

- **Generational Wealth Concentration.** The boomer generation amassed incredible wealth and retained it. They sit in places of influence and leadership. They are living longer. Holding power longer. This created frustration for younger millennials and Gen Xers struggling post-university to find jobs, acquire homes, pay down debts. The dynamic fueled movements (good and bad) seeking to rebalance power structures and access to opportunity.

- **Post-COVID Disruption.** The pandemic broke old systems. Remote work exploded. Digital transformation accelerated. People had time to reflect. To reimagine. To reinvent. The fuel necessary for a new spark arose. People considered a different way. A different path. Getting outside the norm and the status quo.

- **Technological Democratization.** Tools became accessible. AI. No-code platforms. 3D printing. Global marketplaces. The barriers to entry collapsed.

- **Rising Populism** Across nations, populism arose. A deep, necessary momentum. Critical mass. The fuel necessary for people to break patterns.

The variables aligned. Those who act now will shape the next decade and the years beyond. This future belongs to builders willing to enter the fire of personal transformation.

The Crucible: Why Reinvention Requires Pain

Reinvention requires fire. Your neural pathways must be rewired. Your belief systems must be challenged.

Books like *Immunity to Change* (Robert Kegan, Lisa Lahey) and *The Practice of Adaptive Leadership* (Alexander Grashow, Marty Linsky, Ronald Heifetz) describe how difficult this is. Adults have developed their neural pathways. Their ways of being. Their belief systems. Their value systems. Even if they are dissatisfied, breaking that pattern is extremely difficult.

But if there is enough dissatisfaction, enough hunger for something new, you have a shot.

This is why the unknowns rising emerge from communities that have experienced pain, loss, displacement, and marginalization. They have already been through the crucible. They have already developed the resilience required to build. As these leaders emerge, they find a world where the barriers have vanished and the tools are within reach.

As these leaders emerge from the crucible, they find a world where the barriers to entry have vanished, replaced by a technological democratization that puts the future of AI within reach of anyone with a backpack and a dream.

The Hardware Revolution: AI in Your Backpack

The democratization is accelerating faster than most people realize. In 2016, Nvidia delivered the DGX-1 to OpenAI when Elon Musk and Sam Altman were building the foundation for GPT models. The system was massive. Expensive. Accessible only to well-funded labs. In 2025, Nvidia released the DGX Spark. Backpack-size. Around $3,000.

Individual developers can now build AI models themselves. Instead of spending thousands in the cloud, they can iterate and innovate in-house. Do almost unlimited testing before deploying at scale.

This democratization by economies of scale is here now. It will move incredibly fast over the next 12 to 24 months. The playing field is leveling in real time.

■ ■ ■

The Builder's Blueprint: Practical Steps

You are no longer waiting for permission. You are stepping into the DIY revolution. Here is your protocol:

1. Audit Your Process
List the tools you already have access to:
- Smartphone with internet

- Free AI tools (ChatGPT, Claude, Gemini)

- No-code platforms (Webflow, Bubble, Shopify)

- Global marketplaces (Etsy, Amazon, Gumroad)

- Crowdfunding platforms (Kickstarter, GoFundMe)

- Social media networks (LinkedIn, Instagram, TikTok)

You have more access than any generation in history. Stop waiting for permission.

2. Identify Your Crucible

What pain have you experienced that others haven't? What problem do you see that others miss? Your unique suffering is your unique insight.

Write it down -

- **The problem I see clearly:**

- **The community affected:**

- **The solution I can build:**

3. Build Your Network Before You Need It

Nepal's revolution succeeded because networks existed before the crisis. Start building now:

- Join online communities in your field

- Attend virtual meetups and conferences

- Reach out to 3 people per week who are solving similar problems

- Share your learning publicly (blog, social media, newsletter)

4. Start Small, Start Now

You don't need a perfect plan. You need a first step:

- Spend 30 minutes learning one new tool this week

- Build a simple prototype of your idea

- Share your work with 5 people and ask for feedback

- Iterate based on what you learn

5. Develop the Five Blueprints

These are the character traits that position you for breakthrough:

- **Be a learner**: Commit to learning one new skill every quarter

- **Be an achiever**: Set small, measurable goals and hit them consistently

- **Be futuristic**: Spend time imagining what could be, not just what is

- **Be strategic**: Think three moves ahead in every decision

- **Have self-assurance**: Trust your unique perspective, even when others don't see it yet

■ ■ ■

The New Movement: From Activism to Invention

The inventors are rising. These are the holy seeds emerging from the stump of the old era to architect the new. They are fueled by past loss and systemic pain. They will build a civilization that reflects the DNA of Heaven. They will steward the stars and leverage the materials of space for the wellness of humanity.

This is the beginning of a revolution that will redefine the future. The disruptive technologies currently emerging—AI, recursive discovery complexes, and decentralized systems—are the practical mechanisms that will turn this vision into reality.

The gates are open. The tools are in your hands. The window is here. Will you step through?

Appendix B: The 24-Hour Launchpad

YOUR RAPID-RESPONSE GUIDE TO MASTERING THE DIGITAL TOOLKIT

"Give us the tools, and we will finish the job."
Winston Churchill (Feb 9, 1941)

The 1 AM Breakthrough

1 AM. MILWAUKEE. OCTOBER 2023. A missed deadline forced me to scramble. I opened ChatGPT and typed: 'Help me brainstorm 20 ways to communicate the value of integrated healthcare to underserved families who distrust medical institutions.' Thirty seconds later, twenty ideas appeared. Three were brilliant—perspectives I would not have reached after hours of manual brainstorming. In that quiet morning, I understood: the tools had changed everything.

The Amplification of the Unknown

This transformation did not require expensive software, venture capital backing, or an advanced degree in computer science. It required only a simple, accessible tool available to anyone with an internet connection.

Within weeks, my entire leadership philosophy shifted. I began using AI as a 24/7 thinking partner to brainstorm communication concepts, test messaging strategies, and conduct root-cause analysis. The technology did not replace my thinking: it amplified it.

Later, through the **gener8tor** accelerator program for Wisconsin leaders, I witnessed this same pattern on a larger scale. I saw department heads with limited budgets successfully compete against established players, and solo creators launch ventures that possessed the professional polish of a full corporate team. **The conclusion:** the new billionaire class is rising because they mastered these tools first.

The Mindset Shift: From Consumer to Creator

To join the "unknowns" who are rising, you must first navigate a fundamental shift in your relationship with technology.

Digital tools trained you to consume. AI trains you to create. The gatekeepers are gone. You no longer need a massive budget to hire a designer, developer, or copywriter. You can prototype, iterate, and launch with tools that cost less than your monthly coffee budget. The barrier to entry has collapsed. Your willingness to test, fail, and learn determines whether you cross the threshold.

The Discipline of the Prototype

The democratization of creation comes with a vital condition: you must adopt a **testing discipline**.

- Your first website may appear amateur.

- Your first AI-generated images will likely miss the mark.

- Your first automated workflows will inevitably break.

These are not failures; they are the learning steps that separate builders from spectators. The tools lowered the barrier. Your willingness to test and iterate determines whether you build wealth or remain stagnant.

The Three Pillars: Your Framework for Building

Your toolkit should focus on three core areas:

1. **Creation Tools**: Generate content, designs, and ideas

2. **Automation Tools**: Scale your efforts without scaling your time

3. **Distribution Tools**: Reach your audience and build your market

Master all three, and you build a sustainable creator business.

■ ■ ■

PILLAR 1: Creation Tools

AI Writing and Thinking Partners

Start Here: ChatGPT (chat.openai.com)
This is your baseline tool for idea generation, content creation, and strategic thinking.
I use ChatGPT daily for:

- Brainstorming communication strategies

- Drafting initial content that I refine with my voice

- Analyzing problems from multiple angles

- Creating outlines for complex projects

Cost: Free version works fine for beginners. Plus version ($20/month) gives you access to more powerful models. Start free. Upgrade when you hit limits.

Alternative: Claude (claude.ai)

Excels at longer, more nuanced conversations and document analysis. Use it when you need deeper reasoning or are working with large amounts of text.

Your First Action (Do This Tonight):

1. Open ChatGPT

2. Type: "I want to start a business helping [your target audience] solve [specific problem]. Give me 10 potential business models I could test with less than $500."

3. Review the ideas

4. Pick one that resonates

5. Ask follow-up questions to refine it

By 9 AM: You'll have a business concept and initial strategy.

Visual Creation Tools

Canva (canva.com)

Democratized design years ago. Their AI features now make it even more powerful. Create social media graphics, presentations, logos, and marketing materials without design training.

Cost: Free version covers most needs. Pro version ($13/month) adds advanced features.

For AI-Generated Imagery: Midjourney (midjourney.com)

Produces stunning results. You access it through Discord, which feels clunky at first but becomes natural with practice.

Cost: Basic plan starts at $10/month.

Practical Use: Create product mockups, social media content, website imagery, and concept art for your ideas.

Your First Action (Do This Tonight):

1. Sign up for Canva

2. Choose a template for Instagram posts

3. Customize it with your message

    4. Download it

By 9 AM: Post your first piece of professional-looking content.

Website and Landing Page Builders

Durable (durable.co)

Builds a complete website in 30 seconds using AI. You answer a few questions about your business, and it generates a professional site with copy, images, and structure.

This is not your final website. This is your testing website. Launch it. Get feedback. Iterate.

Alternative: 10Web (10web.io)

Similar AI-powered website building with more customization options.

For Landing Pages: Systeme.io (systeme.io)

All-in-one platform. Build pages, collect emails, sell products, and run email campaigns from one tool.

Cost: Free tier supports up to 2,000 contacts.

Your First Action (Do This Tonight):

    1. Go to Durable or 10Web

    2. Answer the setup questions (5 minutes)

    3. Review the generated site

    4. Make one improvement

    5. Publish it

By 9 AM: You have a live website with your business idea.

Video Creation Tools

Descript (descript.com)

Edit video by editing text. Record yourself talking, and Descript transcribes it. Delete words from the transcript, and it removes those sections from the video. Add text, and it generates AI voiceover.

Cost: Free tier includes limited transcription. Creator plan is $24/month.

For Short-Form Content: Opus Clip (opus.pro)

Takes long videos and automatically creates short clips optimized for Tik-Tok, Instagram Reels, and YouTube Shorts.

Your First Action (Do This Tonight):
1. Record a 5-minute video on your phone explaining one thing you know well

2. Upload it to Descript (free account)

3. Edit out the mistakes by deleting text

4. Export the video

By 9 AM: Post your first video to LinkedIn.

■ ■ ■

PILLAR 2: Automation Tools

Creation tools help you build. Automation tools help you scale.

Workflow Automation

Zapier (zapier.com)
Connects different apps and automates repetitive tasks. When someone fills out a form on your website, Zapier can automatically add them to your email list, send a welcome message, and create a task in your project management tool.
Cost: Free tier includes 100 tasks per month. Paid plans start at $20/month.
Alternative: Make (make.com)
More complex automation capabilities at a lower price point.

Your First Action (Do This Tonight):
1. Sign up for Zapier

2. Create a "Zap" that sends you an email when someone mentions your name   on Twitter

3. Test it

By 9 AM: You have your first automation running.

AI-Powered Project Management

Taskade (taskade.com)

Combines task management with AI assistance. Generate project outlines, create workflows, and organize your work with AI support.

Cost: Free tier available. Pro plan is $10/month.

Email Marketing Automation

Beehiiv (beehiiv.com)

Makes newsletter creation simple. Their AI writing assistant helps you draft content, and their automation features handle subscriber management.

Cost: Free tier supports up to 2,500 subscribers.

<u>Your First Action (Do This Tonight)</u>:

1. Start a weekly newsletter sharing one lesson you learned

2. Use Beehiiv's AI to help draft the first issue

3. Write down 10 friends to send it to

By 9 AM: Send your first newsletter.

■ ■ ■

PILLAR 3: Distribution Tools

You can create the best product in the world. If no one knows about it, you have nothing.

Social Media Management

Buffer (buffer.com)

Schedule posts across multiple platforms from one dashboard. Create a week of content in one sitting, schedule it, and focus on engagement.

Cost: Free tier supports 3 social channels. Paid plans start at $6/month per channel.

SEO and Content Optimization

Surfer SEO (surferseo.com)
Analyzes top-ranking content for your target keywords and guides you to create content that ranks. You don't need to be an SEO expert. The tool shows you exactly what to include.
Cost: Plans start at $89/month. Worth it if content marketing is your primary strategy.

Community Building

Circle (circle.so)
Build your own community. Move your audience off social media platforms you don't control and into a space you own.
Cost: Plans start at $49/month.

■ ■ ■

The Manufacturing Revolution: Beyond Digital

Digital tools dominate this appendix because they have the lowest barrier to entry. But the physical world is also being democratized.

3D Printing and Prototyping

Shapeways (shapeways.com)
Design products and have them 3D printed on demand. No need to buy expensive equipment or hold inventory. Upload a design, and they manufacture and ship it.
Tinkercad (tinkercad.com)
Free, browser-based 3D design tools. Learn basic 3D modeling in an afternoon.

Print-on-Demand Manufacturing

Printful (printful.com)

Integrates with e-commerce platforms to manufacture and ship custom products. Design a t-shirt, mug, or poster. When someone orders it, Printful makes it and ships it. You never touch inventory.

Cost: No upfront fees. You pay per order.

Global Marketplaces

Alibaba (alibaba.com)

Connects you with manufacturers worldwide. Source products, customize them with your branding, and launch a physical product business with minimal capital.

The barrier: Research, communication, and quality control.

The opportunity: Massive.

■ ■ ■

Staying Current: The Habit That Matters Most

Tools evolve rapidly. What works today might be obsolete in six months. New tools emerge weekly.

You need a system to stay informed without drowning in information.

Recommended Newsletters:

Superhuman AI (superhuman.ai)

Weekly summaries of AI tools across categories: website building, video editing, project management, finance, education, design, art generation, business, marketing, and productivity.

Ben's Bites (bensbites.co)

Daily AI news and tools.

The Rundown AI (therundown.ai)

AI news in 5 minutes.

AI Tool Report (aitoolreport.com)
Weekly tool reviews.

Your Learning System:

1. Subscribe to two AI newsletters

2. Follow five AI innovators on Twitter/X or LinkedIn

3. Test one new tool each month

4. Document what works and what doesn't

■ ■ ■

The Testing Discipline: Your Competitive Advantage

Tools are worthless without action.

Your competitive advantage comes from testing faster than others. Most people read about tools and do nothing. Some people buy tools and let them sit unused. A tiny fraction actually test, learn, and iterate.

That tiny fraction builds the wealth.

Your Testing Framework:

Week 1: Choose and Learn
- Pick one tool from this appendix

- Watch tutorial videos

- Read the documentation

- Understand the basics

Week 2: Create Your First Project
- Build something simple

- Don't aim for perfection

- Finish it

Week 3: Get Feedback
- Share your work with five people

- Ask specific questions

- Listen to their responses

Week 4: Iterate and Improve
- Make one significant improvement based on feedback

- Launch version 2

- Repeat the cycle

This four-week cycle builds your skills faster than any course or certification. You learn by doing. You improve by shipping.

■ ■ ■

The Tools You Don't Need (Yet)

Beginners make a common mistake: they buy too many tools too soon.
You don't need:
- Expensive design software like Adobe Creative Suite

- Complex CRM systems

- Advanced analytics platforms

- Premium versions of every tool

Start with free or low-cost options. Upgrade only when you hit clear limitations.
Your constraint is execution, not tools.

The Real Investment: Your Time and Attention

Every tool in this appendix costs less than $100 per month. Most cost nothing. **The real investment is your time and attention.**
You must commit to:

- Learning new interfaces

- Watching tutorials

- Testing features

- Failing repeatedly

- Iterating constantly

This investment pays compound returns. Skills you build with one tool transfer to others. Confidence you gain from shipping one project fuels the next. The network you build while learning opens doors you cannot yet see.

■ ■ ■

From Tools to Business: The Bridge

Tools don't build businesses. You build businesses using tools.
The difference matters.
Don't fall in love with the tools. Fall in love with the problem you're solving. Use tools to solve it faster, cheaper, and better than anyone else.
Ask yourself:

- What problem am I solving?

- Who has this problem?

- How can these tools help me reach them?

- What iis the simplest version I can test this week?

Answer these questions. Pick your tools. Start building.

Your 24-Hour Launch Plan

The democratization of technology means that the gap between a prophetic vision and a market-ready prototype has collapsed. You no longer need permission, a large team, or significant capital to start; you only need the discipline to execute.

Phase 1: Your 24-Hour Sprint

The goal is not perfection, but momentum. This plan is designed to take you from concept to a live digital presence in one evening.

Tonight (The 3-Hour Build):

Hour 1: Strategy & Clarification.
- Open an AI interface (ChatGPT, Claude, or Gemini).
- Generate 10 business ideas based on your "lived problems".
- Select one and refine the mission with follow-up prompts.

Hour 2: Visual Identity.
- Create a Canva or Adobe Express account.
- Design a simple logo concept.
- Draft 3 social media posts that communicate your "why".

Hour 3: Digital Launch.
- Use a rapid website builder like Durable or 10Web.
- Publish your site and share the link with 3 trusted friends for a "soft launch".

By 9 AM Tomorrow:
- Post your first piece of social media content to announce your intent.
- Directly message your website link to 10 potential stakeholders.
- Collect and document initial feedback to inform your next iteration.

Phase 2: The 30-Day Mastery Audit

Success is determined by your "testing discipline". Commit to mastering three specific tools this month to move from a consumer to a creator.

   My Three Mastery Tools:

_____ (e.g., Prompt Engineering for Research)

_____ (e.g., No-Code Automation for Operations)

_____ (e.g., AI-Assisted Content Design)

   Set a reminder for 30 days from now. Review your progress, celebrate your build, and select your next three instruments.

■ ■ ■

The Prophetic Dimension: Tools as Stewardship

Joseph interpreted dreams and implemented systems that saved an empire. Daniel received visions and mastered the governance of a foreign kingdom to influence its future. God provides tools for a divine reason.

   The AI platforms and no-code builders are the instruments required to fulfill your calling in this era. Your stewardship of these tools determines the scale of your impact.

Key Takeaway: Master the Tools, Master the Future

The emerging billionaire class does not possess a higher intellect or better pedigree than you; they simply master the tools first. While others research, they test. While others plan, they ship.

   The same tools used to launch million-dollar businesses from bedrooms and coffee shops are accessible to you right now. The future belongs to those who have the courage to build it.

Start building tonight.

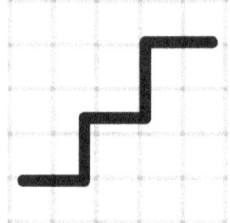

Appendix C: The Inventor Reformation

BIBLICAL BLUEPRINTS FOR SUPERNATURAL INNOVATION

THE **INVENTOR REFORMATION** IS the spiritual return to the original mandate of creation. While the *Industrial Revolution* centralized power in the hands of gatekeepers, this Reformation dismantles those gates through the democratization of Artificial Intelligence. We are not witnessing a mere economic shift. It is the restoration of the systems architect.

The Pattern Hidden in Plain Sight

In early 2004, while sitting in an Austin coffee shop, I read the story of Joseph through a new lens. I realized that Joseph was a systems architect, not just a dreamer. He designed national supply chains, built emergency reserve infrastructures, and managed predictive planning models that saved empires.

Joseph was an inventor. His life is the field manual for the current reformation. The Bible is populated with builders who blended supernatural insight with practical execution. These are the mental models for the AI era.

Ten Biblical Blueprints for Purpose-Driven Innovation

1. Joseph in Egypt: The Systems Architect

The Challenge: A looming fourteen-year cycle of abundance followed by catastrophic famine with no existing infrastructure to manage the crisis.

The Innovation: Joseph created a national supply chain and distribution network through predictive resource management.

Modern Application: Predictive analytics for food security; climate adaptation infrastructure; AI-driven logistics.

The Supernatural Layer: Divine insight revealed data patterns that human analysis could not perceive.

2. Bezalel and Oholiab: The Master Craftsmen

The Challenge: Constructing a sacred space (the Tabernacle) in a resource-scarce wilderness with no existing templates.

The Innovation: Bezalel was filled with the Spirit to possess supernatural skill in metallurgy, stone carving, and woodcraft.

Modern Application: Industrial design; advanced manufacturing; robotics; user experience (UX) architecture.

The Supernatural Layer: Technical proficiency can be a direct result of spiritual empowerment.

3. Boaz: The Ethical Entrepreneur

The Challenge: Providing for marginalized immigrants within a social system that typically excluded them.

The Innovation: Boaz integrated radical social equity into his harvest operations, protecting the vulnerable while maintaining a profitable enterprise.

Modern Application: Fair-trade supply chains; inclusive hiring algorithms; B-Corp structures.

The Supernatural Layer: Business decisions carry prophetic weight for future generations.

4. Solomon: The Wisdom-Driven Builder

The Challenge: Establishing a global brand and a sustainable economy for a rising nation.

   The Innovation: Leveraging strategic alliances and architectural excellence to attract international trade and attention.

   Modern Application: Global brand strategy; strategic M&A; thought leadership; international business development.

   The Supernatural Layer: Seeking wisdom as the primary "product" leads to the accumulation of secondary wealth.

5. The Proverbs 31 Woman: The Portfolio Entrepreneur

The Challenge: Maintaining economic security and community influence across multiple industries.

   The Innovation: She operated agricultural, retail, and real estate ventures simultaneously with high integrity.

   Modern Application: E-commerce; real estate investment; content creation; social enterprise.

   The Supernatural Layer: A reverence for the Creator serves as the foundation for entrepreneurial stamina.

6. Nehemiah: The Civic Innovator

The Challenge: Rebuilding a collapsed infrastructure in fifty-two days while facing intense political opposition.

   The Innovation: He mobilized a demoralized population through visionary leadership and resource secured from the highest levels of government.

   Modern Application: Urban renewal; GovTech; infrastructure development; public-private partnerships.

   The Supernatural Layer: Significant civic projects require a foundation of fasting and intercession.

7. Lydia: The Marketplace Missionary

The Challenge: Funding the expansion of a new movement across international borders.

The Innovation: Lydia leveraged her luxury goods business (purple cloth) to provide the capital and hospitality necessary for mission work.

Modern Application: Mission-driven startups; patronage models; funding networks for emerging leaders.

The Supernatural Layer: Business success is often a positioning move by God for broader Kingdom impact.

8. Abraham: The Generational Architect

The Challenge: Building a lasting legacy and wealth in foreign lands while navigating complex geopolitical treaties.

The Innovation: Managing a decentralized, cross-regional enterprise built on a covenant of faith.

Modern Application: Family offices; generational wealth transfer; long-term impact investing.

The Supernatural Layer: Wealth is the physical manifestation of a spiritual covenant.

9. Tabitha (Dorcas): The Designer for the Marginalized

The Challenge: Serving an overlooked demographic (widows) in a society without a social safety net.

The Innovation: Using design and textile skills to restore dignity through high-quality practical provision.

Modern Application: Affordable design; fashion for social good; services for underserved markets.

The Supernatural Layer: Generosity of this magnitude can unlock miraculous "resurrection" power in a community.

10. The Women of Luke 8: The Strategic Patrons

The Challenge: Sustaining a world-changing movement that lacked institutional backing.

The Innovation: A diverse group of wealthy women (Joanna, Susanna, and Mary) supported the mission out of their private means.

Modern Application: Angel investing; crowdfunding; mission funding networks.

The Supernatural Layer: Financial partnership is a spiritual alignment with the Messiah's mission.

The Great Shift: Industrial vs. Reformation

This shift in perspective is critical for understanding the mechanics of the new era; the following table illustrates the fundamental differences between the old, centralized model of wealth creation and the emerging decentralized system of the Inventor Reformation we see today.

The Industrial Revolution (Centralized)	The Inventor Reformation (Decentralized)
Focuses on centralized power and capital.	Focuses on decentralized tools and access.
Wealth is accumulated by a few gatekeepers.	Wealth is created by a vast army of "unknowns."
Value is extracted from the community.	Value is created for the community.
Success is measured by valuation and exit.	Success is measured by lives changed and healed.

Table C.1: The Unknown's Toolkit for Rapid Systems Innovation

Frontiers for Innovation: Three Pillars of Impact

The Great Shift from extraction to creation is more than just a theoretical comparison; it is the powerful engine powering the next wave of world-changing innovation across these three crucial frontiers:

1. **Health Innovations:** Healing broken systems through AI-powered diagnostics and 3D-printed medical devices that bring expert care to underserved populations.

2. **Education Innovations:** Unlocking potential through AI tutors and virtual reality that provide personalized instruction to anyone, regardless of geography.

3. **Resource Innovations:** Stewarding creation through next-generation energy systems and "waste-to-value" technologies that create sustainable, local jobs.

Building upon these frontiers requires a technological catalyst capable of matching the speed of divine revelation; this is the specific role of **Generative AI** in the current reformation. These tools do more than simply improve efficiency: they democratize access to high-level expertise and enable the "unknown" to innovate at a velocity that was previously reserved for the elite.

The Catalyst: Generative AI Acceleration

Generative AI is the catalyst for the holy seed. It democratizes expertise and enables the 'unknown' to innovate at a velocity previously reserved for the elite.

Healthcare: Restoring the Human Connection

In the domain of health, generative AI acts as both a diagnostic and administrative force:

- It analyzes medical imagery with superhuman precision to ensure accurate diagnostics.

- It generates personalized treatment plans tailored to the specific data of each patient.

- It automates the administrative tasks that currently consume the time of providers.

- It translates complex medical information into multiple languages to increase global access.

- It predicts systemic health risks before they escalate into localized crises.

Education: Unlocking Individual Potential

Within the sphere of learning, AI serves to personalize the experience of every student:

- It creates customized curricula specifically designed for individual learning styles.

- It provides immediate, actionable feedback on student work to accelerate mastery.

- It generates practice modules precisely tailored to close identified skill gaps.

- It translates educational content across linguistic borders to reach the unreached.

- It simulates complex, experiential learning scenarios for practical, real-world application.

Resource Management: Mastering Global Stewardship

For those called to steward creation, AI offers a new level of strategic mastery over physical systems:
- It models complex scenarios to inform high-stakes decisions and minimize waste.

- It optimizes resource systems for maximum resilience and operational efficiency.

- It designs new materials with specific, required properties for sustainable development.

- It analyzes environmental data to detect emerging threats to the ecosystem.

- It generates elegant, data-driven solutions to historically unsolvable problems.

These capabilities are not mere technical upgrades, they are the mechanisms that empower the **holy seed** to steward solutions at a planetary scale. By automating the mundane, the creator is freed to focus on the supernatural, bridging the gap between a problem that matters and a solution that heals.

■ ■ ■

The Prophetic Call: Building for Eternity

Our goal here has been to inspire you through these biblical blueprints on how supernatural innovation can unleash human flourishing. The rising unknowns that are responding to God's commission will have an opportunity to release similar impact and take on these type of greater works:

- Joseph did not merely rescue a nation from famine; he secured the messianic promise.

- Bezalel did not simply construct a tent; he forged the very dwelling place for the Divine Presence.

- Your modern endeavors—the startup you launch, the code you write, the research you pioneer—are your contemporary "Tabernacles," conduits for a purpose far grander than mere commerce or discovery.

The future is here. The exponential power of AI and emerging technologies are the new, potent tools in your arsenal. The window for a profound new billionaire class, one defined not just by wealth, but by eternal impact, stands wide open. The ancient blueprints, the universal principles of building a legacy that outlasts the market cycles, have all been laid out.

The only remaining question: **what will you build for eternity?**

Appendix D: The Family Factor

RECLAIMING THE UNIT OF GENERATIONAL CHANGE

THE PATH FOR THE rising "unknowns" was never designed for the lone wolves. It is a mandate to reclaim the family as the primary unit of economic and spiritual transformation. We have entered a convergence of three historic forces that offer a once-in-a-century opportunity for families who understand the shift.

The Convergence: Why This Matters Now

1. **The Great Wealth Transfer:** We are currently witnessing the largest transfer of assets in human history.

2. **Democratized Creation:** AI tools and decentralized networks allow families to build global businesses from their kitchen tables without institutional permission.

3. **Institutional Decay:** The "social contract" of the industrial age,

promising security in exchange for compliance, has broken down as college costs explode and corporate loyalty vanishes.

Rarely do these forces align in a single generation. When they do, families either rise together or fracture permanently. Consider the scale of the shift currently before us as we approach 2048. Right now, the largest wealth transfer in human history is underway. Baby Boomers control 51.4% of all wealth in the United States, approximately $124 trillion in assets set to change hands by 2048.

Generation	Projected Inheritance	The Opportunity
Baby Boomers	$124 Trillion (Controlled)	Establishing the baseline for legacy.
Gen X	$39 Trillion	The bridge between legacy and innovation.
Millennials	$46 Trillion	Reinvesting in decentralized systems.
Gen Z	$15 Trillion	Leveraging native tech fluency for impact.

Table D.1: The Great Wealth Transfer (Estimated through 2048)

Gen X will receive the largest short-term windfall, averaging $1.4 trillion per year over the next decade. But Millennials will inherit the most over the full 25-year period.

Here's what most analysts miss: This is not just about money. This is about intellectual property, business ownership, real estate, and most critically, the transfer of entrepreneurial knowledge and social capital. If we treat this inheritance as a ledger of digits rather than a repository of values, we will lose the very soul of the wealth we seek to preserve.

To understand how to steward this moment, we must look past the balance sheet and toward a deeper architecture of legacy, one built on the foundations of my own family's "Value Add."

■ ■ ■

The Fajita Pizza Principle: Love as Legacy

The smell of sizzling fajitas in a South Texas hotel kitchen defined my childhood. My father, Arturo Serna Sr., created his signature "Fajita Pizza" not for a business plan, but because his three sons loved it. Wealth transfer does not begin with documents; it begins with a father who sees his children and creates something excellent for them. That kitchen became my first classroom in legacy.

This is the essence of **Social Capital**. While my father never built a global restaurant empire, he successfully transferred the high-yield mindset that work has dignity and creativity is a form of love. The next economic revolution will not be won by those with the largest accounts, but by the families who prioritize these "holy seeds" of wisdom over mere financial figures.

The Shift: From Institutions to Micro-Communities

For seventy years, society outsourced family formation to institutions. We delegated character to youth programs and spiritual development to one-hour weekly classes. The lie of the industrial age was simple: surrender formation, and you will be rewarded with stability. The Inventor Reformation reverses this trend, moving power back to the household.

The Industrial Model (Centralized)	The Inventor Model (Decentralized)
Focuses on corporate loyalty and job titles.	Focuses on family name and generational vision.
Children learn via a standardized curriculum.	Children learn via "Apprenticeship" alongside masters.
Families act as isolated consumer units.	Families act as "Kingdom Outposts" and collaborators.

Table D.2: The Strategic Shift from Institutional Outsourcing to the Decentralized Inventor Model.

When technology democratizes creation, when AI and automation handle routine tasks, when individuals can build global businesses from their kitchen tables, **the family becomes the ultimate competitive advantage**.

The Biblical Pattern: Family as the Primary Institution

God never intended institutions to replace families. He designed the family as the primary vehicle for transferring wisdom, wealth, and purpose across generations.

Proverbs 13:22 makes this explicit: *"A good person leaves an inheritance for their children's children."*

Notice the timeframe. Not just your children. **Your children's children.** This is multi-generational thinking. This is legacy architecture.

Deuteronomy 6:6-7 lays out the method: *"These commandments that I give you today are to be on your hearts. Impress them on your children. Talk about them when you sit at home and when you walk along the road, when you lie down and when you get up."*

The transfer happens in the ordinary rhythms of life. At the dinner table. On the drive to practice. During weekend projects. In the daily texture of shared existence.

This was never curriculum. This was always apprenticeship.

■ ■ ■

The Biblical Models

Abraham to Isaac to Jacob (Genesis 12-50)

God's covenant promises flowed through family lines. Each generation received the blessing, wrestled with it, and passed it forward. The result shaped nations.

Lois to Eunice to Timothy (2 Timothy 1:5)

Faith transmitted through maternal mentorship. A grandmother and mother prepared a young man for global leadership. Paul recognized this pattern and honored it.

David to Solomon (1 Kings 1-11)

Imperfect fathers can still transfer wisdom. David's failures taught Solomon what not to do. His successes showed what was possible. The temple David envisioned, Solomon built.

In each case, the family served as the incubator for world-changing impact. In Scripture, God rarely entrusts world-changing vision to individuals. He entrusts it to bloodlines.

The Micro-Family Office: Managing Vision, Not Just Money

The ultra-wealthy use "family offices" to manage their assets, but the unknowns rising can adopt the same principle. A family office is not just about a portfolio; it is about managing **knowledge, relationships, and vision.** In an age where tools scale instantly, trust becomes the rarest and most valuable currency.

By forming **Micro-Communities**—small networks of three to five families—the unknowns can pool their diverse expertise. One family may master AI, another healthcare, and a third strategic capital. Together, they create a collaborative ecosystem where ideas scale with mutual benefit.

How to Build Your Micro-Community:

- **Identify:** Look for 3–5 families who share your generational values.

- **Rhythm:** Establish consistent touchpoints, such as monthly dinners or quarterly retreats.

- **Share:** Distribute tools, connections, and knowledge freely within the group.

- **Collaborate:** Launch a shared venture, such as a micro-school or a community garden.

- **Accountability:** Pray together and hold each other to the "Seek First" Kingdom strategy.

You cannot do this alone. No family is an island.

. . .

Practical Exercise: The Family Vision-Casting Guide

Set aside three hours this week to map your family's intellectual and spiritual capital.

1. **Remembering:** Share one story of a family member who modeled excellence and one lesson learned from a family failure.

2. **Envisioning:** Discuss what your family wants to be known for and what problems you feel called to solve three generations from now.

3. **Planning:** Identify one concrete action to take in the next 90 days that develops a family member's unique gifts.

4. **Praying:** Ask for wisdom in stewardship and for your family to be used as a channel of blessing to the nations.

5. **Recording:** Write this vision down and revisit it annually as a family covenant.

The Clarion Call: Building a Dynasty

You are not merely making money; you are making history.

Every great civilization was built on the foundation of strong families. And every collapse began with their breakdown. The next generation of unknowns will not be lone wolves. They will be sons and daughters carrying forward the wisdom of their ancestors.

The choice is yours to make right now: will you allow your wealth to be scattered to the wind, or will you steward a legacy that outlives your lifetime and changes the world?

Appendix E: The Monetization Path

TURNING DIVINE VISION INTO PRACTICAL REVENUE

VISION WITHOUT REVENUE IS a hallucination. Innovation without monetization is a stewardship failure. This appendix is the bridge between your calling and the marketplace. We are moving from inspiration to income because the Kingdom requires resources to scale its reach. These pages are designed to move you from inspiration to income within 90 days.

The Principle of the House: Starting With What You Have

The story of the widow and the oil in **2 Kings 4** serves as the ultimate entrepreneurial mental model. When faced with crushing debt, she believed she had nothing. The prophet asked a pivotal question: "What do you have in your house?" Her answer—a single jar of oil—became the asset base for a national turnaround.

Your Inventory Audit

Before seeking external capital, you must audit the "oil" already in your possession:

- **Acquired Skills:** The technical mastery you forged in the "trenches" of your career.

- **Relational Networks:** The high-trust capital you've built through years of integrity.

- **Earned Credibility:** Your reputation, which functions as the primary currency in a decentralized economy.

- **Democratized Access:** Your ability to leverage AI to do the work of a ten-person department.

Four Paths to Capital and Growth

There is no "one size fits all" strategy for monetization. The following table compares four proven paths to fund your "holy seed" innovation:

PATH	CORE MODEL	BEST FOR	PRIMARY ADVANTAGE
Bootstrapping	Reinvested Revenue	Service businesses, low-cost startups	Full ownership and control
Crowdfunding	Community Validation	Physical products, social causes	Market validation before launch
Angel Investors	Strategic Partnership	High-growth, capital-intensive ideas	Mentorship and network access
Acquisition (ETA)	Legacy Building	Transitioning existing businesses	Immediate cash flow and systems

Table E.1: Strategic Funding Paths for the Rising Unknown.

Crowdfunding Resources:
- Kickstarter

- Indiegogo

- Republic (equity crowdfunding)

Angel Investing Resources:
- AngelList

- Gust

- Local angel investor networks

Key Resources for ETA:
- **"Buy Then Build" by Walker Deibel**The definitive guide to entrepreneurship through acquisition. Covers search, financing, due diligence, and transition.

- **Search Fund Accelerator**Training and community for aspiring acquisition entrepreneurs.

- **BizBuySell**Largest marketplace for businesses for sale.

- **SBA 7(a) Loan Program**Government-backed loans for business acquisition.

The ETA Path: Buying Instead of Building

Entrepreneurship Through Acquisition (ETA) is the path most "Unknowns" may overlook. Do not build from zero if you can buy from one hundred. With the Great Wealth Transfer underway, thousands of sound businesses are looking for a successor. This is the 'Legacy Rescue.' You take a fundamentally strong operation and inject it with the 'Unknown's Toolkit'—AI, digital velocity, and Kingdom vision. Consider:

- **Immediate Revenue:** You buy cash flow on day one rather than building it from zero.

- **Lower Risk:** Historical financial data allows you to see exactly where innovation can add value.

- **The Innovation Play:** You take a fundamentally sound business and modernize it using AI and digital marketing.

■ ■ ■

The Truth About Fundraising: Lessons from $19M+

Capital follows conviction. In raising over $19M, I learned that investors do not fund programs; they fund missions.

- **Narrative over Numbers:** Your story is the engine; the data is the fuel.

- **Alignment over Asking:** You are not a beggar; you are an opportunity for an investor to align their capital with eternal impact.

- **Value Precedes Capture:** Money follows a sequence. You must identify a problem worth solving and validate the demand before you can capture sustainable revenue.

The 90-Day Execution Roadmap

Use this condensed timeline to move from a concept to your first paying customer.

- **Weeks 1 to 2: Insight.** Audit your internal assets and define one core problem you are uniquely positioned to solve.

- **Weeks 3 to 4: The Minimum Viable Offer (MVO).** Design the simplest version of your solution that delivers real value.

- **Weeks 5 to 8: Validation.** Reach out to ten potential customers and secure your first "yes" through early-adopter pricing.

- **Weeks 9 to 12: Scale.** Refine your offer based on feedback and develop a marketing plan to reach a wider audience.

Breaking the Barrier of Fear

Fear of failure or rejection is the primary barrier to revenue. In the Kingdom economy, fear is not a stop sign; it is often a sign that you are stepping into a purpose larger than yourself.

- **Clarity:** Pray for eyes to see the "oil" already in your house.

- **Courage:** Act on revelation even when the full path is not yet visible.

- **Stewardship:** Remember that money follows value, and value follows obedience.

Three Prayers to Break Through Fear

Prayer 1: For Clarity

"God, show me what You've already placed in my hands. Help me see the oil in my house. Give me eyes to see what others miss."

Prayer 2: For Courage

"God, give me the courage to take the first step. Not reckless action, but faithful obedience. Help me move even when I can't see the full path."

Prayer 3: For Provision

"God, You are Jehovah Jireh, my provider. I trust You to multiply what I offer. I trust You to bring the right customers, partners, and resources at the right time."

■ ■ ■

You Have Everything You Need to Begin

The world needs what you're building. Your family needs the provision it will create. The Kingdom needs your obedience to the call.

Money follows value. Value follows obedience. Obedience follows revelation.

The window is open. The tools are in your hands. The oil is in your house.

Now, go.

Sell the oil. Build the storehouse. Fund the movement. Your obedience is the only thing standing between the problem and the solution.

Appendix F: Where Calling Meets the Cutting Edge

SEEING WHAT'S COMING

I SAT IN A parking lot in Milwaukee, Wisconsin, watching history unfold on my phone screen. The SpaceX Starship and Super Heavy stack launched from Starbase in South Texas, just an hour and a half from McAllen, where I grew up. Tears filled my eyes as I watched that massive rocket defy gravity, carrying with it the audacious dream of making space exploration economically viable through reusability.

This was not just engineering. This was prophecy made manifest.

The same passion that drew me to astronomy in high school, the same curiosity that made me fall in love with calculus and physics, the same wonder that made me look up at the stars and see God's infinite creativity—all of it converged in that moment. I was witnessing the future being built in real time, launched from the soil of my homeland.

Emerging technology is the mechanism that pulls the future into the present, transforming the 'someday' of God into the 'today' of the builder.

Enoch: The Prototype of Prophetic Innovation

Before we explore the technologies reshaping our world, we need a framework. Not just a business framework or a technology roadmap, but a spiritual prototype for how to navigate the future.

Enter Enoch.

> *"Enoch walked faithfully with God; then he was no more, because God took him."*
>
> Genesis 5:24, NIV

Enoch's story is one of the most mysterious in Scripture. Unlike other patriarchs defined by conquest or wealth, **Enoch's legacy is transformation through intimacy with God.** He is the prototype for the Inventor Reformation. He did not react to the present; he responded to the future.

Enoch as a Prototype of Innovation

- **Future-Seer.** Enoch received visions of what was to come (Jude 14-15), modeling how leaders can anticipate shifts before they arrive. He did not react to the present. He responded to the future.

- **Adaptive Walker.** His walk with God was not static. It was a continual process of learning, adapting, and being reshaped by divine wisdom. Every step forward required recalibration. Every revelation demanded transformation.

- **Dimension Navigator.** Ultimately, he mastered the art of walking in the earthly realm while being governed by heavenly intelligence.

What Enoch Teaches the Unknowns Rising

The unknowns rising must adopt Enoch's posture. You cannot build the future by clinging to the past. You cannot navigate emerging technologies with outdated mindsets. You cannot steward prophetic vision without the discipline of daily intimacy with God.

Enoch walked with God for 300 years. Not a single dramatic moment. Not one viral breakthrough. Just consistent, faithful steps in the same direction. That's the pattern for those who will shape the next era.

The technologies in this appendix are not just tools. They are invitations to walk with God into territories that don't yet exist. They are opportunities to see what He is building and join Him in the work.

■ ■ ■

The Technology Landscape: Where the Unknowns Will Build

Technology is a lens into the ideas in the mind and heart of humanity. Emerging technologies are a futuristic window into a world that will come. **Future founders will win as they develop their prophetic lens and build the discipline and habit to live from the future.**

According to McKinsey's 2025 Technology Trends Outlook, we are witnessing a convergence of over a dozen frontier technologies that will reshape business, society, and human potential. These are not isolated innovations. **They are interconnected systems that amplify each other, creating exponential possibilities.**

While not exhaustive, this list provides a representative sample. The convergence of these frontier technologies is the infrastructure of the new Kingdom economy.

1. Artificial Intelligence and Machine Learning

What's Happening:
AI has moved from research labs to everyday tools. Large language models like ChatGPT, Claude, and Gemini are democratizing access to intelligence. Computer vision is enabling machines to see and interpret the world. Predictive analytics are transforming decision-making across industries.

Why It Matters:
AI is the most significant technological shift since the internet. It amplifies human capability, automates routine tasks, and creates entirely new categories

of work. Those who master AI tools now will have a 5-10 year advantage over those who wait.

Where the Unknowns Can Build:

- **AI-Powered Solutions for Underserved Communities:** Most AI development focuses on wealthy markets. Massive opportunity exists in building AI tools that serve low-income communities, non-English speakers, and regions with limited infrastructure.

- **Faith-Integrated AI Applications:** AI tools that help churches manage operations, pastors prepare sermons, and ministries scale their impact. The intersection of faith and technology is wide open.

- **AI for Small Business:** Most small businesses can't afford data scientists or AI consultants. Tools that make AI accessible to mom-and-pop shops, solo entrepreneurs, and family businesses will create enormous value.

- **Ethical AI Frameworks:** As AI becomes more powerful, the need for ethical guardrails grows. Unknowns with strong values can build frameworks, tools, and consulting practices that help organizations deploy AI responsibly.

Key Skills to Develop:
Prompt engineering, basic Python programming, understanding of machine learning concepts, data literacy, ethical reasoning.

Resources:

1. Fast.ai (free courses)

2. Google AI Essentials

3. OpenAI Cookbook

4. Hugging Face tutorials

2. Biotechnology and Health Innovation

What's Happening:
CRISPR gene editing is making genetic modification accessible. mRNA technology (tested through COVID vaccines) is opening new frontiers in disease

ntiers in disease treatment. Personalized medicine is moving from concept to reality. Longevity research is accelerating.

Why It Matters:

Healthcare is broken. Costs are unsustainable. Access is unequal. Chronic diseases are epidemic. Biotechnology offers solutions that could fundamentally reshape how we prevent, diagnose, and treat illness.

Where the Unknowns Can Build:

- **Community Health Tech:** Tools that bring preventive care, health education, and early diagnosis to underserved communities. Mobile clinics powered by AI diagnostics. Telemedicine platforms designed for low-bandwidth environments.

- **Mental Health Innovation:** The mental health crisis is global. Apps, platforms, and services that make therapy accessible, affordable, and culturally relevant will save lives and build wealth.

- **Nutrition and Wellness:** Personalized nutrition based on genetic profiles, microbiome analysis, and lifestyle data. This is moving from luxury to necessity.

- **Faith-Based Health Models:** Integrating spiritual care with physical health. Building clinics, apps, and services that treat the whole person—body, mind, and spirit.

Key Skills to Develop:

Basic biology and genetics, understanding of healthcare systems, regulatory knowledge (FDA, HIPAA), data privacy, empathy and cultural competence.

Resources:

1. Khan Academy (biology and health courses)

2. NIH resources on precision medicine

3. WHO guidelines on community health

3. Clean Energy and Climate Solutions

What's Happening:

Solar and wind energy are now cheaper than fossil fuels in most markets.

Battery technology is improving rapidly. Electric vehicles are reaching price parity with gas cars. Carbon capture and storage technologies are emerging.

Why It Matters:

Climate change is not a future threat. It's a present reality. Communities are being displaced. Crops are failing. Extreme weather is increasing. Those who build solutions will not only create wealth—they will save lives.

Where the Unknowns Can Build:

- **Distributed Energy Systems:** Solar microgrids for rural communities. Battery storage solutions for areas with unreliable power. Energy cooperatives that give communities ownership of their power.

- **Sustainable Agriculture:** Vertical farms. Regenerative agriculture practices. Technologies that help small farmers increase yields while reducing environmental impact.

- **Climate Adaptation Tools:** Apps and services that help communities prepare for and respond to climate impacts. Flood prediction. Drought management. Heat wave response.

- **Faith-Driven Climate Action:** Mobilizing churches and faith communities to adopt clean and smart energy, reduce waste, and advocate for creation care. Building the theological and practical frameworks for this movement.

Key Skills to Develop:

Basic understanding of energy systems, project management, community organizing, policy literacy, systems thinking.

Resources:

1. Project Drawdown

2. Clean Energy Resource Teams

3. Interfaith Power & Light

4. Space Technology and Exploration

What's Happening:

Private companies like SpaceX, Blue Origin, and Rocket Lab are making space access cheaper and more frequent. Satellite technology is enabling global internet coverage. Space manufacturing and mining are moving from science fiction to business plans.

Why It Matters:

Space is not a luxury. It's infrastructure. Satellites provide communication, navigation, weather monitoring, and disaster response. The next generation of global connectivity will come from space.

Where the Unknowns Can Build:

- **Satellite Data Applications:** Using satellite imagery for agriculture, disaster response, urban planning, and environmental monitoring. The data exists. Most communities don't know how to use it.

- **Space Education and Inspiration:** Programs that bring space science to underserved schools. Curriculum that uses space exploration to teach STEM. Experiences that inspire the next generation of engineers and scientists.

- **Space-Enabled Services:** Businesses that leverage satellite internet (like Starlink) to serve remote communities. Telemedicine. Distance learning. E-commerce in areas previously unreachable.

- **Theological Exploration of Space:** As humanity becomes a multi-planetary species, we need theological frameworks. What does it mean to be made in God's image on Mars? How do we steward creation beyond Earth?

Key Skills to Develop:

Basic physics and orbital mechanics, data analysis, GIS (Geographic Information Systems), storytelling and education, theological reasoning.

Resources:

1. NASA educational resources

2. SpaceX updates and launches

3. Satellite imagery platforms (Sentinel Hub, Google Earth Engine)

5. Blockchain and Decentralized Systems

What's Happening:

Blockchain technology enables secure, transparent, decentralized record-keeping. Cryptocurrencies are creating new forms of money and value transfer. Smart contracts are automating agreements without intermediaries. DAOs (Decentralized Autonomous Organizations) are experimenting with new governance models.

Why It Matters:
Traditional financial systems exclude billions of people. Banks are slow, expensive, and often predatory. Blockchain offers an alternative: peer-to-peer transactions, transparent governance, and financial inclusion for the unbanked.

Where the Unknowns Can Build:
- **Financial Inclusion Tools:** Crypto wallets and payment systems designed for people without bank accounts. Remittance services that reduce fees for immigrants sending money home.

- **Supply Chain Transparency:** Blockchain-based systems that track products from origin to consumer. This matters for fair trade, ethical sourcing, and combating fraud.

- **Decentralized Identity:** Systems that give people control over their own data and identity. This is critical for refugees, undocumented immigrants, and anyone without traditional ID.

- **Faith-Based DAOs:** Decentralized organizations that fund kingdom work, support missionaries, and coordinate global ministry efforts without traditional hierarchies.

Key Skills to Develop:
Basic cryptography, understanding of blockchain architecture, smart contract basics, community governance, ethical reasoning about decentralization.

Resources:
1. Ethereum.org (educational resources)

2. Coinbase Learn

3. MIT OpenCourseWare on blockchain

6. Quantum Computing

What's Happening:
Quantum computers use quantum mechanics to solve problems that are impossible for classical computers. They're still in early stages, but progress is accelerating. Companies like IBM, Google, and startups are racing to build practical quantum systems.

Why It Matters:
Quantum computing will revolutionize drug discovery, materials science, cryptography, and optimization problems. It will break current encryption methods and require entirely new security frameworks.

Where the Unknowns Can Build:

- **Quantum Literacy:** Most people don't understand quantum computing. Educators, writers, and communicators who can explain it will be valuable.

- **Post-Quantum Cryptography:** As quantum computers threaten current encryption, new security methods are needed. This is a massive opportunity for those with cryptography skills.

- **Quantum Applications:** Once quantum computers are practical, they'll need applications. Those who understand both quantum mechanics and real-world problems will build the first killer apps.

- **Ethical Frameworks:** Quantum computing raises profound questions about privacy, security, and power. Unknowns with strong values can shape how this technology is governed.

Key Skills to Develop:
Basic quantum mechanics, linear algebra, programming (Python, Q#), systems thinking, ethical reasoning.

Resources:

1. IBM Quantum Experience (free access to quantum computers)

2. Microsoft Quantum Development Kit

3. Qiskit tutorials

7. Augmented and Virtual Reality

What's Happening:
AR overlays digital information on the physical world (think Pokémon Go or Apple Vision Pro). VR creates fully immersive digital environments. Mixed reality blends both. These technologies are moving from gaming to education, training, healthcare, and remote work.

Why It Matters:
The way we interact with information and each other is changing. Flat screens are giving way to spatial computing. This will transform education, collaboration, and entertainment.

Where the Unknowns Can Build:
- **Educational Experiences:** VR field trips for students who can't afford travel. AR apps that bring textbooks to life. Immersive history lessons that let students experience the past.

- **Training and Simulation:** VR training for dangerous jobs (construction, emergency response). Medical simulations for healthcare workers. Soft skills training in realistic scenarios.

- **Virtual Churches and Communities:** As people become more distributed, virtual gathering spaces will matter. Building VR churches, prayer rooms, and community centers that feel real.

- **Therapeutic Applications:** VR for PTSD treatment, phobia therapy, and pain management. AR for physical therapy and rehabilitation.

Key Skills to Develop:
3D modeling, Unity or Unreal Engine, UX design for spatial computing, storytelling, empathy and user research.

Resources:
1. Unity Learn

2. Meta Quest developer resources

3. Apple Vision Pro developer tools

8. Robotics and Automation

What's Happening:
Robots are moving out of factories and into homes, hospitals, and farms. Drones are delivering packages and monitoring infrastructure. Autonomous vehicles are getting closer to widespread deployment. Automation is reshaping every industry.

Why It Matters:
Labor shortages, aging populations, and dangerous work environments create demand for robots. But automation also threatens jobs and raises questions about dignity, purpose, and economic justice.

Where the Unknowns Can Build:

- **Robots for Good:** Autonomous systems that serve underserved communities. Delivery drones for medical supplies in remote areas. Agricultural robots that help small farmers compete.

- **Human-Robot Collaboration:** Tools and frameworks that help humans and robots work together effectively. This is about augmentation, not replacement.

- **Ethical Automation:** Consulting and frameworks that help organizations automate responsibly. How do you deploy robots without destroying livelihoods? How do you retrain displaced workers?

- **Robotics Education:** Programs that teach kids and adults how to build, program, and work with robots. This is the literacy of the future.

Key Skills to Develop:
Basic robotics, programming (Python, ROS), mechanical design, systems integration, ethical reasoning about automation.

Resources:

1. ROS (Robot Operating System) tutorials

2. Arduino and Raspberry Pi projects

3. MIT OpenCourseWare on robotics

Explore the 2025 Report for a Deeper Study here:

- McKinsey Technology Trends Outlook 2025

■ ■ ■

The Integration Challenge: Where Technologies Converge

The breakthrough is in the synthesis. Joseph didn't just understand grain; he understood logistics, economics, and prophecy. You must become an *Integration Specialist*. AI + biotechnology = personalized medicine. Blockchain + clean energy = decentralized power grids. Robotics + space = autonomous exploration. AR + education = immersive learning.

The unknowns rising will not specialize in just one technology. They will become integration specialists, people who see connections others miss and build solutions that span multiple domains.

This requires:

- **Broad Learning:** Don't go deep in one area too quickly. Explore widely first. Understand the basics of multiple technologies before specializing.

- **Systems Thinking:** See how technologies interact. How does AI change healthcare? How does blockchain enable clean energy? How do robots and VR work together?

- **Problem-First Mindset:** Start with real problems, not cool technologies. What needs fixing? What communities are underserved? What injustices need addressing? Then find the right technology mix to solve it.

- **Collaborative Networks:** No one can master everything. Build relationships with specialists in different fields. Create teams that combine diverse expertise.

. . .

The Enoch Posture: How to Stay at the Cutting Edge

Technology changes fast. What's cutting edge today is obsolete tomorrow. How do you stay current without burning out? How do you discern what matters from what's hype? Let's return to Enoch. He walked for 300 years before he graduated.

Walk Daily: Consistent, small steps beat sporadic sprints. Spend 30 minutes every day learning something new. Read. Watch. Experiment. Build the habit of continuous learning.

1. **Stay Close to the Source:** Enoch walked with God. You must stay connected to the One who sees the future. Pray over your learning. Ask God what He's building. Listen for His direction.

2. **Adapt Constantly:** What worked last year won't work next year. Be willing to pivot. Be willing to unlearn. Be willing to start over when necessary.

3. **Think Generationally:** You're not building for next quarter. You're building for your grandchildren. Choose technologies and projects that have long-term kingdom impact.

4. **Transcend When Ready:** Enoch didn't cling to earth. When it was time to move to the next dimension, he went. Be willing to let go of projects, technologies, and even identities when God calls you forward.

The Prophetic Assignment: Build What Heals

These technologies are not neutral. They can heal or harm. They can liberate or oppress. They can restore dignity or strip it away. The unknowns rising carry a prophetic assignment: build what heals.

Use AI to serve the overlooked. Use biotechnology to cure the sick. Use clean energy to restore creation. Use space technology to inspire wonder. Use blockchain to include the excluded. Use quantum computing to solve the unsolvable. Use AR/VR to educate the unreached. Use robotics to dignify labor.

This is not about getting rich. This is about stewarding the moment God has given you.

■ ■ ■

The Future Is Being Built Right Now

The future is not something that happens to you; it is something you build with Him. That SpaceX launch I watched from a Milwaukee parking lot was not just a rocket. It was a declaration: the future belongs to those who build it. **Now, go build what heals.**

You don't need permission. You don't need perfect conditions. You don't need elite credentials.

Use the code to serve the overlooked. Use the satellites to reach the unreached. Use the algorithms to restore justice.

The window is open. The tools are ready. The Father is waiting.

The technologies in this appendix are your tools. The Enoch posture is your framework. The prophetic assignment is your calling.

Walk.

Epilogue: This Is Not Prosperity Gospel

OBEDIENCE OVER OPULENCE

CRITICS WILL ATTEMPT TO label this a prosperity gospel. They will assume I am promising wealth without the weight of the cross. They are mistaken. This is not a theology of comfort; it is a theology of commission. We are not seeking a life of ease; we are seeking a life of obedience that happens to be well-resourced for the sake of the Kingdom.

What Prosperity Gospel Says vs. What This Book Says

Let's define the core differences.

- **Obedience over Opulence.** The Prosperity Gospel says God wants you rich; the Kingdom says God wants you obedient. Abraham didn't leave Ur for a paycheck; he left because he heard a Voice.

- **Purpose over Protection:** The Prosperity Gospel promises an exemption from trials; the Kingdom promises a purpose within them. Faith is not a shield from suffering; it is the fire that refines you to endure it.

- **Systems over Scorn:** The Prosperity Gospel judges the poor for a lack of faith; the Kingdom judges the systems that keep them bound. Our call is to dismantle institutionalized evil and build architectures of dignity.

The reality is that God's pioneers often suffer. The call is not a guarantee of comfort. It is a guarantee of purpose.

The Conditions of Prophetic Fulfillment

Prophecy is not magic or a guarantee. It is an invitation. But invitations come with conditions. You must RSVP. You must show up. You must participate.

To see the vision of the "Unknowns" manifest, six conditions must be met:

1. **Obedience:** You must act on the word. If I had stayed silent in October 2020, the vision would have passed to someone else. God will accomplish His purposes with or without us.

2. **Timing:** God's timing is often a deliberate delay. Joseph waited thirteen years from the dream to the palace. If he had been promoted a year early, he would not have possessed the character required to save a nation.

3. **Testing:** The vision must be challenged. My transition from a CEO role in 2025 was not a failure of the vision; it was the birth of the next chapter. Testing is the proof that the vision is real.

4. **Community:** Prophetic vision is communal. Moses needed Aaron; Paul needed Barnabas. If you are the only one who sees your vision, it may be ambition. When a community confirms it, it is a commission.

5. **Character:** God will not promote you until your character can sustain your calling. Promotion without character leads to destruction. The "coal from the altar" burns to purify before the promotion arrives.

6. **Sacrifice:** You will lose things. Abraham lost his country; Paul lost his

status. You will lose comfort and security, but you will gain an eternal legacy.

■ ■ ■

The Warning: Wealth Without Character Destroys

Wealth is not the goal. Character is. Wealth without character destroys.

- **Solomon** was the wisest and wealthiest king in history, but he compromised. He married foreign wives. He worshiped their gods. He oppressed his people with heavy taxes. His kingdom split after his death. His legacy was tarnished.

- **Nebuchadnezzar** was the most powerful king of his era, but pride consumed him. He declared himself god. God humbled him. He ate grass like an animal for seven years until he acknowledged the Most High.

- **Ananias and Sapphira** lied about their wealth. They wanted the reputation of generosity without the sacrifice. God struck them dead.

- **The rich young ruler** had wealth, but he loved it more than he loved God. Jesus told him to sell everything and follow Him. He walked away sad.

Wealth is a tool. A test. A responsibility. If you love it, it will destroy you. If you steward it, it will bless others.

The new billionaire class will not love wealth; they will steward it. They will treat capital as a tool for restoration, not a trophy for the ego.

The Purpose: A Sacred Calling to Heal the World

You are not called to become a billionaire for your own sake. That path is empty. Your true mandate is a sacred one: to **heal the world**, to solve problems that crush the human spirit, and to embrace the iron law of the collaborative ecosystem: **you rise only by lifting others.**

A vision from October 2020 was seared into my consciousness. The new wave of leaders rising will possess no self-seeking attitude. Their very existence is about change that benefits all of humanity. They will build not just from strategy, but from the supernatural realm, guided by the non-negotiable values of their Maker. The zeal of the Lord will consume them.

Their work will be a testament to this calling. They will create inventions that solve real problems—health innovations that snatch lives from the brink, education solutions that shatter ceilings of potential, and resource innovations that secure true sustainability. Their paradigm shifts completely: *they will not extract wealth from communities; they will generate wealth for communities*.

This is the stark chasm between the old billionaire class and the new.

- The old guard accumulated; the new distributes.

- The old hoarded; the new shares.

- The old built walls; the new builds bridges.

Your destiny is clear: You are not called to reinforce the broken system of the old class. **You are called to pioneer the new.**

■ ■ ■

A Primer on Prophetic Partnership

Prophecy is not magic, nor is it a mechanism for fortune-telling or manipulation; it is the divine revelation of God's purposes so that His people may partner with Him to bring them to pass. For the younger generation of "unknowns" entering the marketplace, understanding this distinction is the difference between a life of superstition and a life of strategic stewardship.

Prophecy Is Conditional

Prophecy serves as an invitation to a specific future, but that future remains contingent upon the human response.

- Prophetic warnings are invitations to repentance.

- The story of Jonah and Nineveh proves that a sincere change in heart can alter a declared outcome or its timing.

- God explicitly states in Jeremiah 18 that His plans to build or uproot are influenced by a nation's obedience or rebellion.

- Biblical prophecy is a divine proposal rather than a guaranteed, fixed destiny.

Prophecy Requires Partnership

God rarely forces His will upon a generation; instead, He invites us to co-labor with Him to see a vision manifest.

- The vision of the "unknowns" rising in the AI era is an invitation that requires a corresponding action.

- While God provides the supernatural vision, the believer must provide the practical obedience.

- Prophetic fulfillment is a collaborative effort involving building, creating, and stewarding.

- A "yes" in the spirit must be followed by a "move" in the natural world.

Prophecy Must Be Tested

The Apostle Paul commanded believers not to treat prophecies with contempt, but to subject them to rigorous evaluation.

- Every prophetic word must be weighed against the immutable truth of the Holy Scriptures.

- True prophecy is identified by the fruit it produces: solutions that heal, wealth that blesses, and communities that thrive.

- A valid vision will always glorify the nature of God rather than elevate human ambition.

- Divine clarity is confirmed through the mouth of multiple witnesses and the validation of a trusted community.

Prophecy Has Guardrails

God does not contradict His own nature; therefore, prophecy will never authorize a violation of biblical ethics or character.

- Any word that encourages the abandonment of integrity or family for financial gain must be rejected.

- The guardrails of the prophetic life include character, sacrifice, community, and divine timing.

- Biblical prophecy values the development of the soul over the accumulation of cash.

- Staying within these ethical boundaries ensures that the "unknown" will not crash under the weight of their own success.

■ ■ ■

The Acceleration: The Genesis Mission

The future has arrived. On November 24, 2025, an Executive Order signed by President Donald J. Trump launched the **Genesis Mission**. This is a prophetic sign in the natural world. By leveraging the National Laboratories and uniting the nation's brightest minds with next-generation AI, the Genesis Mission aims to double American scientific productivity within a decade.

This represents a shift from "human time" to "machine time." We are transitioning from a research engine limited by human capacity to an autonomous discovery complex. This shift changes every technological equation on Earth.

Why this matters for the Unknowns: The infrastructure for the "new billionaire class" is being built right now. Compute is the new oil. The unknowns rising today will build on this discovery complex. They will steward innovations in biotechnology, space exploration, and quantum science to heal the world.

Systems that improve recursively do not slow down; they compound. This is the moment the future truly begins.

■ ■ ■

The Bones Are Living

I think of my Gen Z mentee in Milwaukee. He was overlooked and underestimated, but he taught himself to build games that heal trauma. He is the "dry bone" that has received the breath of life.

Ezekiel 37:3 asks: "Son of man, can these bones live?" I answer: "Sovereign Lord, You alone know." Then I watch as the army stands. The "Unknowns" are rising. They are the holy seed remaining in the land. They are the Josephs and Daniels of the AI era.

The Invitation: "Here Am I, Send Me"

God is raising an army that refuses to be defined by the binary of socialism or secular capitalism. They are governed by a third way: the Kingdom of Heaven. They will rise not because they are credentialed, but because they are consecrated.

The window is open. The tools are in your hands. The invitation is blood-bought.

Will you say yes?

May you see what God is doing. May you hear His call. May you rise by lifting others and build the systems that will transform our world.

Go. Build the systems that heal. Create the wealth that restores.

The world is waiting for the Unknowns to rise.

`Arturo Serna Jr.`
`Milwaukee, Wisconsin`
`2025`

Acknowledgements

I count it a unique honor to partner with God as a vessel allowing the vision of *The Unknowns Rising* to pour forth into a world standing at a digital and spiritual crossroads. This book would not have reached your hands without the giants who stood in the gap, the pioneers who provided the tools, and the family who anchored my soul when the winds of the unknown blew the hardest.

The Spiritual Foundations

I must first thank the spiritual giants: Bob & Leslie Long, Ronnie & Gail Long, and Jim & Jean Hodges. At key moments in my life, you spoke words of affirmation and direction that helped me decipher my calling within God's broader design. You commissioned me "to the nations," and by your example, you modeled how to hear the voice of God with clarity and conviction. This book is a reality because of the anchor you helped me drop into the depths of His promise.

To the community of World Impact Ministries in Pewaukee, Wisconsin—under the graceful leadership of Pastors David and Beverly Rehfeld—I have no words to describe the magnitude of my gratitude. You welcomed my family as we responded to the Abrahamic call "to go," and in the scary, dark places of the transition, you were a light that allowed the vision of the unknowns to take shape in my spirit. I am excited to see how this message reaches the nations and builds a community of fiery pioneers who see beyond the four walls of safety to love others with abandonment.

To the tribal mothers guided by Roselyn Staples and Deniese Redd: your counsel, prayers, and trust have been a lifeline. In the shaking moments of uncertainty, your steady dose of faith and love shaped the conditions for this truth to see the light. You remind us all of what an obedient community of Christ's disciples can truly be.

The Intellectual and Creative Architects

To my colleagues, Elijah Low and Dr. Alan Lockett: your research and work in Artificial Intelligence helped me ground this prophetic word in the technical inflection point we now inhabit. You helped me move past the hype and anchor myself in substance, allowing me to size the opportunity and appreciate the urgency of this era.

To Christy McFerren, who handled the book cover design with masterful precision: thank you for letting me interrupt your international travels to keep this project on its divine timeline. It was refreshing to work with a master of her craft who truly "gets" the creative imagination. And to Tonya Serna, for reviewing early mock-ups and shaping my belief in what could be, your eye for beauty and love of excellence never cease to amaze me.

The Serna Legacy and The Beta Community

To my father and mother, Arturo and Maria Serna: your unconditional love and support humble me. You poured your lives out so that I could blaze a new path and achieve a new height for the Serna tribe. I cherish the warmth you provided during the summer of 2025, which reconnected me to my design and purpose. This book took flight because of the seed of promise you both planted. To Val and Frank Serna, thank you for the phone calls that made me feel seen and heard. Your entrepreneurial journeys helped confirm that the "Unknowns Rising" vision was indeed emerging from the heart of God.

To my community of beta readers—Karen Serna, Roselyn Staples, Ana Cheng, Deniese Redd, Francisco Serna, John Serna, and Evelyn Christy—*muchas gracias, amados*. Your perspectives guided me through the iterations of this project and deepened my clarity. You helped me shift this work from good to great. John, this father very much appreciated your input as a representative of your generation; may it bring the Lord much glory as it goes forth.

I am eternally indebted to the love of my life, Karen Joy Serna. Your steadfast commitment to my leadership, vision, and dream keep me going. I thank you for being my intercessor, advocate, and friend when I needed to press through. The early morning and late nights going through the drafts of this book are a beautiful testament to your affection and belief in me. You continue to be my special gift from Father God to journey this adventure called life.

Finally, to the brilliant minds I have learned from along this journey—Adria Dunn, Wes Chapman, Tarja Stephens, Julia McCoy, and Brendan Mc-Cord—keep blazing new horizons. You remind us to keep the best of humanity at the center of design. To the friends who remained steady through the uncertain: you have been the wind behind my sails. We are stepping through the gate now, and I am excited to witness the hand of God doing a new thing over the nations. I am running with all my might alongside you to see this wonderful thing spring up before us all.

About the Author

ACTIVATING THE NEW BILLIONAIRE CLASS THROUGH FAITH, TECH, AND PROPHETIC VISION

Author, Arturo Serna Jr.

ARTURO SERNA JR. IS a prophetic voice for the next generation of faith-driven entrepreneurs and a catalyst for the unknowns rising into their God-given purpose. He was born in the United States and raised between two worlds, Mexico and the Rio Grande Valley of South Texas, and he learned early what it means to navigate cultural barriers, family expectations, and the complexity of bicultural identity. His father, a hotel chef who created the *Fajita Pizza* out of love for his three sons, modeled the kind of generational vision that shapes Art's work today. This was innovation born from love, excellence expressed through craft, and a legacy built through the strength of family.

Art holds a BS in Astronomy from the University of Texas at Austin and an MS in Management of Technology from the University of Texas at San Antonio. He is a certified AI professional and cybersecurity leader who has dedicated over two decades to building organizations, raising millions in funding, and mentoring innovators at the intersection of technology, faith, and social impact. His career spans leadership roles at Teach For America, United Way, and multiple healthcare and education organizations. He has raised over $19 million in support of social impact initiatives and built strategic partnerships across corporate, government, and nonprofit sectors while developing frameworks for adaptive leadership in times of rapid technological change.

But his most important work began with a prophetic encounter in October 2020.

Three months after arriving in Milwaukee, Wisconsin, Art received a vision that would become this book. It is a roadmap for the new billionaire class emerging from unexpected places because God showed him a generation of creators, inventors, and builders who would reshape industries, democratize wealth, and leave a legacy of generational impact.

This book is the fruit of that encounter and a testament to the "Unknowns" who are being called to the forefront.

Art is the founder of **Cosmos Renewed**, where he equips unlikely entrepreneurs to discover their unique strengths and build sustainable, faith-centered ventures. He is an ordained minister, a speaker, and a strategy advisor who bridges the gap between practical business execution and spiritual calling. He lives in Milwaukee with his wife Karen, a veteran homeschool educator who runs their Kratos Academy, and their two children. His family remains his greatest treasure and his constant source of inspiration. Art believes the future belongs to the perpetual learner, the faithful steward, and the unknown who refuses to stay hidden.

Connect with Art

For speaking engagements, podcast interviews, or collaborative projects, you can visit Art's profile at https://unknownsrising.com/ or scan the QR code below.

Unknowns Rising Community Page

www.ingramcontent.com/pod-product-compliance
Lightning Source LLC
Chambersburg PA
CBHW060430130626
46555CB00005B/2288